COLOUR HEALING

COLOUR HEALING

AMBIKA WAUTERS
AND GERRY THOMPSON

To Theo Gimbel

Thorsons
An Imprint of HarperCollins*Publishers*
77–85 Fulham Palace Road,
Hammersmith, London W6 8JB
1160 Battery Street
San Francisco, California 94111–1213

Published by Thorsons 1997

3 5 7 9 10 8 6 4

©Ambika Wauters and Gerry Thompson 1997

Ambika Wauters and Gerry Thompson assert the moral right to
be identified as the authors of this work

A catalogue record for this book
is available from the British Library

ISBN 0 7225 3340 3

Printed and bound in Great Britain by
Caledonian International Book Manufacturing, Glasgow

CONTENTS

ACKNOWLEDGEMENTS

This book has had a special energy of its own. I wish to thank my co-author Gerry Thompson and my publisher Wanda Whiteley for their kindness and patience in seeing it into print. My thanks to Colin Peel, my greengrocer, who supplied me with endless supplies of delicious fruit to make the colourful drinks mentioned in the book. To Sue Bell for showing me My True Colours, and to Rachel Kelly for developing a wonderful business with colour. As always my thanks to my friends Josh Enkin, Allison Jackson-Bass, Mary Jardine, Ann Carter, Chrissie Pickin and Sandy Cotter. My thanks to my sister, Nita and her daughter, Jamie, for their support and friendship, and to my father Bill and my aunt and uncle, Loris and Ben and my cousins David, Paula and Tani. I have an interesting and colourful family to whom I am indebted for their creativity and enthusiasm for life. To my mother, who taught me that nothing in nature ever clashes, I wish to offer my thanks for so many gifts. My thanks to Susan Mears, my agent, whom I wish to acknowledge for her guidance and good counsel.

The publishers would like to thank Jillie Collings for her suggestion for the title of this series, *Principles of ...*

INTRODUCTION

A human being cannot live without colour.

Colour is inextricably bound up with light. All our cells and the cells of all plants and animals and living things are dependent on light and affected by even the most subtle changes in the qualities of light. During the winter months, when for days on end the sky is grey and colourless, we can easily get depressed. But this is only the simplest example of how we are affected by light and colour.

Colour is magic. It comes to us most strikingly through flowers and sunsets and moonlight and tropical sea anemones. If we have forgotten to wonder at this beautiful world of colour, we may have let the duties and obligations of our everyday existence weigh too heavily upon our shoulders, with worries gnawing away at our thoughts and our emotions, then draining away our life energies and creating ill-health.

A WORLD OF COLOUR

We live in a world of colour. It is all around us in every object we see, in both nature and man-made things, but often we respond to it with a muted sensitivity, taking it for granted. This can come from constantly being surrounded by its richness wherever we look. The moment we leave our normal environment and travel to a new landscape, the first thing we will notice will be differences in the colours and textures. Likewise, when we are deprived of the beauty of clear skies for too long, we come to notice that we are affected by the dullness that envelopes us. And if we live too long under artificial light, we naturally crave the beauty and brightness of nature, with its integrity of true colours and natural light.

Ambika remembers, many years ago, taking a train from the airport to the city of London. Seated next to her was a young man, whom she discovered had been in India for some time. He marvelled at what he saw as the miracle of green in the English countryside. He spoke of this colour with such feeling that she realized that it was touching him deeply. At the time Ambika was not able to appreciate this reaction, for it all seemed rather ordinary to her, but she has since come to comprehend more fully the profundity and significance of the effect the colours had on this man.

Those of us who live among particular colours and patterns of light can easily become insensitive to their enchantment and magic. When we begin to awaken our senses to the beauty, mystery and profound qualities of colour, we become sensitive to its healing properties. Colour is synonymous with joy and with life. It also reflects our love for life and is a symbol for our emotions, at the best and worst of times. How we use it, wear it or otherwise experience it is essential to our personal expression and identity. The colours that we make use of speak volumes about our attitudes, our behaviour and what life means to us, if we can only understand the code and realize its meaning. Colour is also an unmistakable code that can tell strangers just what we are feeling and what our attitudes are.

Recently, a particularly sensitive client wrote about her experience with colour. She performs a highly skilled job in computers, and has a highly developed sense of subtle energies as well. She wrote this:

> The sense of colours arises in me from certain sounds and particular touches. To me, the final chord of a particular Liszt prayer, for instance, can amaze me with a sense of liquid, swirling orange. The memory of Polynesian drumbeats and a flickering fire, the pattern of footprints from sandals and Pacific waves breaking behind me together produce extraordinary rolls of orange, red and purple. To me, colours always have this intense, vivid, liquid nature.

This woman also mentions that she sees colours when she has deep sexual experiences. When she is relaxing, she also sees colours around her; life is richer for her when she is in the countryside, or when she is travelling, because then colours are even more intense to her. Her experiences are unusual because they are so deep and profound. But we could all sense colours with this degree of intensity and awareness, if we tuned in to the vibration of the colour around us. We all have the capacity to feel something that is so close to our soul. This book offers you that opportunity: to explore different ways of colour healing.

WHAT THIS BOOK CONTAINS

In ancient days, the vital importance of colour and its conscious use was formally recognized and used as a means of healing in temples. The priests and priestesses used it to help soothe the spirit when troubled, or to aid the physical body – balancing the internal energy system by either cooling inflammation or warming energy-deprived areas of the body. Treating people with colour, in fact, goes back to the earliest of times, when it was thought that the sun was literally the source of life, as well as of light and heat – so colours were considered to be the sun's vital messengers. Colour was considered a primal part of ritual, of healing and of spiritual practice, as indeed it remains in some traditional cultures today. (The distinguished history of colour healing is looked into further in Chapter 1.)

In order to grasp the profundity of colour's potential for healing us, it is useful to understand a little about how it is that colour has its effect on us. Chapter 2 describes this process and explains why it is that the various colours have such radically different effects and qualities. It also shows how these healing effects reach into all aspects of our lives, from our physical health to our emotional well-being, even our patterns of behaviour and basic personality traits.

Chapter 3 introduces the many different approaches that are in use today to bring healing through colour. Broadly speaking, there are two main categories of people who have developed these approaches. First there are the pioneering workers purely in the field of colour itself, who have developed a variety of complementary health methods using colour. Their work is innovative and exciting, and they are on the leading edge of medical technology; it may, however, be many years before most of these ideas are brought into the mainstream. Secondly, there are many new health therapies that are used in hospitals and clinics, which incorporate the use of colour and light. Modern medicine, in fact, is taking up colour healing and giving it new applications through the use of highly sophisticated technology. Light-based technology has implemented some major developments – colour can now, for instance, save the life of a premature baby, or help to remove cancerous cells without cutting away vital parts of the body. Whether your preference is for conventional or complementary health methods, as you read this book you will be surprised at how many roles colour has to play in modern healing, even though these 'new' ways of healing really embody the ancient principles in a different form. (The Appendix contains reference material for those readers who wish to explore any of these individual approaches in more depth.)

Colour healing is one of the major possibilities for the way forward for medicine. It combines work with subtle energies and with powerful technology, which touch us at the core.

Chapter 4, by contrast, describes simple methods to use yourself, to deal with your own particular health problems or to enhance your own physical and emotional well-being and happiness. This chapter begins with a guide to which colours relate to which conditions of health, and then a variety of self-help techniques is introduced. First you will read about the practical and physical methods, such as applying coloured light, eating foods of appropriate colour, or combining colour techniques with other therapies such as reflexology. You may well be amazed at how well you feel after you have had a session under the lights.

Then we describe the 'inner' methods of working with colour, such as visualization and meditations using different colours. As well as helping with physical and emotional health issues, and rebalancing and aligning your energy fields, these methods provide an opportunity for spiritual development; for the world of colour is the reflection of the soul. It radiates the light of the spirit, and expresses that deep inner light through all that you do and in all that you express. It asks to be taken into the highest realms of consciousness. Again, the reference material in the Appendix will enable further in-depth work in any of these methods.

A NEW APPROACH

In treating illness today, conventional medicine relies heavily on drugs and surgical methods. This book will be valuable, then, for those people who wish to explore other possibilities.

It looks into the many different ways that colour can contribute to your health and well-being, and it offers you a new approach that is gentle, safe and effective.

Colour is something everyone can relate to. It offends no one. It crosses many boundaries and opens people up to a new world of personal expression, clarity and illuminations. It goes to the depths of who we really are.

Human beings have been granted a unique grace – the opportunity to grow and develop slowly throughout life. The more slowly this development towards maturity, the greater the potential to develop a higher degree of consciousness by absorbing the lessons of experience. Learning lessons from the magical world of colour can play an enormous part in this process of growth, self-discovery and evolution, for each being on our planet.

Whether colour healing is used in hospital, ancient healing temples or in the modern home, it has a profound role to play in our lives. It offers a non-invasive and highly refined form of healing, while it soothes and satisfies the spirit. It comes from the place where life itself originates, and where we will go when we cease to be, as physical beings. Because it is so familiar to our spirit, colour helps us to know ourselves and express our deepest thoughts and feelings with both clarity and light.

We sincerely hope that your life will be touched and enriched by the exciting encounter with colour healing on which you are about to embark.

THE HISTORY OF COLOUR HEALING

From the most ancient of times of human existence, colour has been of vital significance. Not only did it give people practical information about plants, animals and seasons, which were very much a matter of life or death, but it seems that the earliest of people developed an awareness of colour beyond this purely pragmatic aspect. Judging from the cave paintings and other artworks that survive from the earliest time, anthropologists know that those who executed them attributed spiritual and earthly symbolism to certain colours, and used these qualities in the first manifestations of shamanistic healing. This most probably developed out of the inherent patterns of colour which their ancestors discerned in nature. These characteristics of specific colours are timeless, and still relevant to the ways used in colour healing today.

The most common colours used in the earliest rituals were red, black and white. Red, for instance, the colour of fire and of blood, has probably always had tremendous power in its associations with danger, and also with taboos in connection with women's monthly cycles. It has been used for ages as a warning not to cross boundaries. It also signifies the presence of life and vitality, and figures prominently in cave paintings of the animals of the hunt. Red was mined from the earth in very early times as ochre, and later extracted from plants such as madder, or drawn out of insects such as cochineal. As time passed, shades of red were also used to dye cloth, and came to play an important role in death ceremonies. Red ochre was sprinkled on graves and painted on the bodies of the dead; as their spirits passed on, those left behind wished that their life energy would be carried with them to whatever lay beyond. Indeed, the Massai of east Africa still dye their robes with red ochre dug from riverbeds; they paint the bodies of warriors with it for initiation, and wash their dead in it before burial. Red is recognized in colour healing as carrying the primary qualities of the life force and energy.

Black was more directly associated with death; death was an ever-present possibility, and the sacrifice of black animals was thought to keep the spirits of the otherworld appeased. In Ireland, even until relatively recent times, it was still believed that a black egg from a black hen had healing power, as did the blood from a black cat. When the moon goddess became a dominant deity, she symbolized death, mystery and divination, and was honoured monthly. She was transformed in the course of the lunar month; at the new moon, and was portrayed as the white goddess of birth, and then became the red goddess of fertility, before returning to black in the waning of the moon. Black is used in colour healing today to absorb negativity.

As humankind evolved from Neolithic times, from relying solely on hunting and gathering to cultivating crops, so the ritual and shamanistic use of colour broadened. The sun came to be embraced as the primary symbol of divinity, and significance was placed on the concept of harvest and fecundity, expressed by the colours green and yellow.

Clairvoyants such as Edgar Cayce maintain that true colour healing originated in Atlantis, and was taken from there to ancient Egypt. Whether one can accept this or not, it is none the less certain that this therapy was developed to a high degree in that latter culture. The Egyptians used temples as healing centres for physical and spiritual well-being throughout the land, specially constructed to channel sunlight in controlled beams. The name of their most holy city, Heliopolis, means 'city of lights'.

The Egyptians used colour in the form of coloured ointments, made by grinding gemstones of the required hue and mixing them with fats or waxes. These were applied to relevant parts of the body. Frescoes which survived show maidens grinding green malachite, mixing it up and applying it to their eyes. Green is used today to soothe the eyes. Science has demonstrated that green is actually the easiest colour for us to see, as its rays fall directly onto the retina, due to its wavelength, while red and blue fall just in front and just behind (Chapter 2 explains this in more detail).

The Egyptians also used yellow beryl stone to cure jaundice, and bloodstone to treat blood disorders and haemorrhage. The Papyrus Ebers records, dating from 1500 BC, also list white oils, red lead oxide, indigo and green copper verdigris mould among its colour cures.

In India, too, healer-priests had a distinct system of colour science. In ancient China colour was included in the development of early medical science, both as an aspect of diagnosis and in cures. For instance, a 'red pulse' was interpreted as indicating 'numbness of the heart', a yellow complexion showed a healthy digestive system, and a green complexion warned of extreme illness and, possibly, imminent death. Even modern Western medicine uses the colour of the complexion as a prominent part of making a diagnosis.

In most ancient cultures, physical healing and spiritual ritual were not separated, as they tend to be in our time, and the use of colour was integral to these activities. Indeed, a considerable degree of uniformity is evident in the significance and use of colours in quite distinct societies and historical eras. The Egyptians, Tibetans and Native Americans have all regarded turquoise as the most sacred of colours, and used it as a symbol of heaven and in the creation of sacred objects and clothing. Purple has often been used to express the majesty and superior standing of emperors and kings. Violet has been associated with prophetic abilities, while orange has denoted a visionary. Red has often been used in initiations, and blue is regarded as the symbol of emotional maturity. Yellow and green have generally been the colours of fertility and harvest.

Early astrologers, who were also concerned with health and well-being, linked the planets inextricably with individual colours – Mars was associated with red, yellow with the sun, white with the moon, green with Mercury, Saturn with indigo, and so on.

When we look at the timeless meanings and effects of colour in the next chapter, we will begin to understand the reasons for all of these traditions.

As time passed, more sophisticated uses of colour in well-being evolved. Around the time of the first millennium, for instance, when the great cathedrals of Europe were being built using the recently evolved methods of Gothic architecture, it was possible to incorporate great and beautiful windows. These were decorated with vibrant coloured glass – not only to illuminate the minds of men and symbolize divine energies, but were used for physical healing as well. The ill and dying were carried into these great buildings, and placed in the pools of light shining onto the floor. There they could absorb the healing effects of the colours, and many stories of healing 'miracles' are on record.

Throughout the medieval era, the doctrine of *humours* dominated European thought on health and its treatment. There were thought to be four elements or humours, and the state of equilibrium between them was considered crucial in consideration of well-being. An imbalance was signified by colour. Black bile was associated with the humour or emotion of melancholy. Too much red blood was thought to be evidence of a sanguine personality. Yellow bile or spleen produced choleric energy, while white represented a phlegmatic personality. This analysis was actually the starting point of the development of modern Western diagnosis. The Chinese, Hindus, Greeks and Romans had all followed the Doctrine of Humours for centuries. Such systems of classified elements have been discerned in all cultures in connection with health matters, and here again colour has been a fundamental consideration. For instance, in the Chinese system of Five Elements, which is still used today, essentially unchanged, as it has been for thousands of years, a person who is angry or irritable is regarded as having an excess of Wood energy: wood is the element that governs the liver, signifying the spring-like flow of life force that is present in the organ when it is healthy; it is associated with the colour green. When the liver is in this state, the influence of green surroundings is part of the classic recommended treatment; in modern colour healing, green light could equally well be used to give peace and to calm the nerves.

In the Middle Ages, too, Paracelsus formulated a methodology for using colours for healing. Unfortunately he was probably too far ahead of his time, and his work did not gain acceptance. He was attacked and scorned, and most of the manuscripts containing his discoveries were destroyed.

Many great and influential figures in history have been bewitched by colour and its effects on our state of well-being – in classical Greece alone, Pythagoras, Hippocrates, Plato, Aristotle and Pliny all tried to explain its mysteries. In the Renaissance era, Leonardo da Vinci was also preoccupied with it. Goethe was extremely preoccupied with colour and its relationship to creativity.

THE NEWTONIAN AGE

The first person to understand how colour works in scientific terms was Sir Isaac Newton, in the 17th century. He discovered the phenomenon of the visible spectrum, and drew diagrams to demonstrate how sunlight can be broken down into bands of different wavelengths, each of which represents one of seven major colours. When he tried to break these down further, he found that it could not be done. The interesting thing is that healers from many of the ancient cultures, such as the spiritual healers of Egypt, India and China, were all aware of the essentially seven-fold nature of colour; so we can say that, in this and many other ways, modern science is confirming what the sages of old knew very well indeed.

Newton also discovered how it is that the lines along which light travels can be bent and refracted. Newton was in fact the founder of modern physics of colour and light.

MODERN TIMES

As we approach the modern era, we see the use of light and colour in healing being integrated with the new, technologically-orientated methods of medicine that came out of the Industrial Revolution, which have come to dominate modern conventional health care. The first book to have been published explicitly on colour therapy is thought to have been *Light and its Rays as Medicine*, by Dr S. Pancoast, published in 1877. It discerned the fundamentally differing effects of red in stimulating and blue in soothing the human body. In 1878, a substantial and influential work entitled *The Principles of Light and Colour*, written by Dr Edwin Babbitt, appeared. By the end of the 19th century it had become possible to separate out distinct elements of pure coloured light, such as infra-red and ultra-violet (UV). In Denmark it had long been observed that skin lesions associated with tuberculosis were far more prevalent in the winter than in the summer; in the 1890s, Niels Finsen experimented with the use of UV light on patients in the winter, and found that it produced remarkable cures. For this pioneering work he was awarded the Nobel Prize for medicine in 1903.

Not long after this, two scientists called Dinash Ghadiali and Harry Spitler developed the new sciences of spectro-chromotherapy, which involved the treatment of the body by way of applied light. They found that lemon-green light was effective for many different kinds of chronic and persistent disorders, and that turquoise was appropriate for more acute conditions. They used purple, scarlet and magenta light for conditions of the heart, circulation and reproduction – purple for correcting over-activity, scarlet for under-activity and magenta for balancing. Indigo light was prescribed for any pain, abscesses and bleeding. D. P. Ghadiali's magnum opus on colour therapy, published in the US in 1933, was *The Spectro Chromemetry Encyclopaedia*. Ghadiali's work was very important to colour healing as it is practised today.

At the time, the work of these men was considered the great advance of the century; however, as time passed the meteoric rise of the use of synthesized medical drugs took over, and research into all other methods was pushed into the background, until very recent decades. More recent and detailed developments in this field will be related in Chapter 3.

8   Colour healing has played its part in the conscious management of human health and well-being through all eras, right up to the present moment. Now let's look at just how this wonderful force for good works to bring such widespread and profound benefits.

HOW COLOUR
HEALING WORKS

Colour is light, and light is life. Without light, there truly is no life on this planet. Without colour, there is no differentiation in form, variety and individuality. Colour is so essential to our existence that we cannot even begin to speculate how things would be without it. Science has discovered the existence of chemical compounds that work in nature purely to differentiate life's creations on the basis of colour – substances such as haemoglobin, melanin, carotene and chlorophyll, all of which are vital to the life force of plants, animals and insects. Yellow and black markings on snakes and insects warn us of their potential danger, and red spots on spiders tell us to keep well away. These colours operate through deep-seated and universally instinctive processes. Colour affects us directly, drawing us towards some things and repelling us from others.

THE MEDIUM OF COLOUR

Colour is the medium through which we perceive light, and are affected by it. The quality of colour may actually occur in the form of the light itself – the dawn or dusk, sunlight or moonlight – or in the objects themselves as pigments.

Flowers, grass, trees and herbs, for instance, all take on the colour of their pigmentation. When humankind began to make use of colour in altering artefacts, the original pigments used were plant dyes. Later, mineral sources began to be used, and then coal tar colours. But the connection with light as the source of colour quality remains; the trees and herbs and flowers lose their pigmentation if grown in the dark, and even the most 'permanent' dyes and pigments are somewhat affected by light.

Here is an exercise that demonstrates some of the basic effects of colour. Look at a blue object, focusing your gaze on it for a few moments. Then find a red object of the same size, and focus on it from the same distance. Switch from one to the other and you will notice how your eyes need to re-adjust when switching attention from the blue to the red. You will also become aware that the red object appears nearer to you than the blue one.

But the effects go a lot further than this. For instance, let's say you dress someone all in white. If you were to measure the person's blood pressure, then expose him or her to red coloured light for five minutes and then measure his or her blood pressure again, you would find that it has risen. Change to blue light for five minutes and the blood pressure will *fall* below the original level.

Colour, in fact, affects minutely the cell behaviour of all bio-chemical structures. Colour therapy practitioners are able to treat a great variety of ailments today, from loss of vitality or SAD (Seasonal Affected Disorder) to more serious or persistent conditions such as eczema, migraine and asthma. Yellow, for instance, is helpful for arthritis sufferers. Turquoise rejuvenates cell structures and aids immunity. Green can destroy harmful cells, such as in cancer.

Colour is a powerful influence on human mood, emotions and atmosphere. Violet, for instance, promotes dignity and self-respect. Most people have some inkling that this is a factor in their choice of home decor, but could take it a great deal further. A small room painted red, for instance, will look much smaller than it really is, but painted blue will appear a lot larger. Furthermore, in a blue room time will seem to pass more slowly; the sort of remark commonly heard there will be, 'Don't worry, there's plenty of time.' Whereas in a red room, 'It's getting late, we must hurry!' will be all the cry.

Different colours will have different effects on the emotions in many other ways. Furthermore, for each individual there will be some colours with which he or she personally will be happier than others. A blue dining-room is likely to give your dinner guests indigestion. A touch of red in the bedroom could be just what you need to spice up your sex life. Colour in clothing offers the same kind of scope for informed choice. You can choose clothes that make you 'feel better', simply because colour produces actual chemical changes in the molecular structure of your body cells. For instance, blue vibrates about eight trillion times each second, while red vibrates at about two thirds of this speed. Children, and others among us who function more intuitively, know about this effect by instinct. They are exploring this when they find brightly coloured toys attractive to play with. Similarly, native peoples living in the tropics are drawn to wear brighter colours which match the energies of their environment.

You could even bring this kind of awareness into choosing a new car. Quite apart from the criteria of self-expression and more abstract qualities, there is the very important aspect of optical and spatial impressions already mentioned. Just look around when you are next out and you will see that blue cars are more often dented than other colours, simply because other drivers who park near them often judge them to be further away than they really are. People nearly always park further away from a red car than a blue one. In fact, scientists have discovered that a red object is actually more brittle than an identical blue one. Hence, blue crash helmets are safer than red ones!

HOW COLOUR WORKS

The great philosophers of the past have tried to explain the qualities, energy and power of colour. Modern science has given a more precise and quantifiable explanation of why different colours affect us so varyingly.

Light is just one form of electro-magnetic radiation, or vibrating energy, as are sound and heat and radio waves. Indeed, modern physics has now accepted that even what we think of as solid objects are actually composed of energy, which is simply vibrating at a distinctive frequency which we associate with 'solidity'. Theo Gimbel, one of the great pioneering figures of modern colour healing, expresses the opinion that, as colour is of a much higher vibration than sound, it consequently has a much more profound impact upon the human being, setting off finer and more powerful chemical changes than sound does. So all those common expressions of ours, such as 'seeing red' or 'feeling blue', are actually an articulate description of changes that are taking place in our bodily field of electro-magnetic energies.

All kinds of vibrating energies are distinguished and explained in their effects and qualities by two closely related criteria or parameters. One is the wavelength, or distance between individual waves of the vibration as they radiate out from their source – which, in the form of natural light, is the sun. The other parameter is the frequency of vibration, which means the number of waves passing a fixed point, say each second. A single particular shade of coloured light has a fixed or constant wavelength and frequency, while white or natural light is a mixture of many wavelengths and frequencies.

We have seen that many civilizations of the past have been intuitively or pragmatically aware of the differing colours within the range of the spectrum; modern technology has made it possible to measure these differences precisely.

Blue, for instance, vibrates at a relatively high frequency, while red vibrates much more slowly; red light is actually denser or heavier than blue. Violet has the shortest wavelength and highest frequency of all. Light travels through space in straight lines, but many peoples have discovered that when sunlight is passed through a glass prism the individual components (of different colours) are bent or 'refracted' to different degrees, producing a spectrum of separate rays, just as happens with light passing through droplets of water in the earth's atmosphere to create what we call a rainbow.

All physical matter both absorbs and reflects light to some degree; objects 'take on' the colour of the component of light that they reflect, and do not appear to possess the colours that they absorb. This is in turn determined by pigmentation. A carrot, for instance, appears orange to us because it contains carotenoids, a type of pigment which absorbs the shorter wavelength rays and reflects the longer wavelength radiation. The same pigment gives salmon or lobster flesh and autumn leaves their distinctive colouring. Haemoglobin is the pigment that colours our blood red, and anthocyacin brings different shades of red to grapes, beetroot and tomatoes.

What we see and describe as a colour, however, is only that part of the spectrum that is reflected off towards us. This information is picked up by tiny sensory rods and cones in the retina of the eye, which absorb minute amounts of chemicals

according to the colour composition of the rays, and send this to the optic nerve, which in turn sends messages to the brain, which makes extremely precise calculations that enable us to make sophisticated colour distinctions. It is thought that this capacity has evolved very significantly since the days of primitive humanity, when, it is thought, people could distinguish only three colours – red, yellow and black. So our ability to distinguish colour, to be affected by it and to use its subtleties, is ever evolving and developing in terms of sensitivity and refinement. Some researchers believe that in due course we will be able to perceive new colours which we cannot at present.

ANALYSING COLOUR

There are three ways of analysing the range of colours. From the point of view of the chemistry of mixing pigments, the primary colours are red, yellow and blue. As even school-children know, these mix to produce the secondary colours – mixing red and yellow gives us orange, yellow and blue produce green, red and blue result in violet. The three primaries together produce black.

However, the physics of colour involve light – the source of colour rather than the inherent colour of objects. And by this analysis, the hierarchy of colours works differently. The three primaries are red, green and blue-violet. When these are blended together, red and green make yellow, green and blue-violet produce light turquoise, and red and blue-violet create magenta.

Thirdly, from the human sensory point of view there are the three conventional primaries of red, yellow and blue, but green is also a first-degree colour; all the other colours come from these four, and they mix to produce grey. Red, orange and yellow form the 'magnetic' end of the spectrum, and have a warming or activating effect. Blue, indigo and violet are at the 'electrical' end of the range, and are calming in effect. Green is in between these in nature and in effect. It is because of these differing vibrational qualities that blind people are often able to distinguish the colour of objects by touch. The visible spectrum, then is:

red
orange
yellow
green
blue
indigo
violet.

In colour healing, these individual components are sometimes known as *rays*. None of the rays from the sun is inherently warm; they only take on their various degrees of heat as an effect of passing through the earth's atmosphere. So the effects of colours as we experience them on Earth are essentially a unique phenomenon.

Each colour also has its own *complementary* colour – the one that is opposite and balancing in its qualities and effects. You can see these by staring at a colour for a while, then closing your eyes and looking at the colour of the after-image. In terms of the healing use of colours, blue balances red, yellow goes with violet and orange with indigo; green is neutral.

HOW COLOUR AFFECTS US

Colour affects us profoundly and in a great number of ways. We will now look at those that are most integral to colour healing.

We instinctively know about the qualities and effects of the different colours, even if this knowledge is often unconscious, and collectively we express it in our vernacular language. We speak of being tickled pink, we see the world through rose-coloured spectacles, or we get caught red-handed. We get into a black mood, act lily-white or sing the blues. We write purple passages, develop green fingers and speak of grey areas in a subject that we are not so sure about. As colour plays such a significant part in our lives, we have woven it into the fabric of our language; it becomes a powerful and popular metaphor for the feelings that we experience, helping us to express them evocatively by association with the relevant hue. Awareness of colour enables us to come to a deeper understanding of life itself. It enriches our language and helps us to refine our communication. Our intuitive awareness of all this leads us also to recognize colourful language, acknowledge colourful experiences and meet colourful characters. When we feel good, we 'lighten up'; we can 'see the light at the end of the tunnel' and feel 'brilliant'!

EMOTION AND BEHAVIOUR

So it is clear that we have some instinctive awareness of the emotional effects of colour. However, most people are not aware of just how profound and how varied these effects are, and how precisely colour can thus be used as an instrument of emotional healing. Modern science is going a long way towards explaining the mechanisms by which these powerful influences operate.

It is interesting how universal an agreement there is between different cultures about the symbology of colour. On the one hand, we know that when ten people look at the colour blue, it is certainly true that they will each have a uniquely personal response to it, as far as their own individual associations vary; indeed, a colour seen and experienced in conjunction with a particularly happy or unhappy moment can continue to evoke that emotional association for decades afterwards, even for life. At the same time there will also always be an underlying universal theme that blue evokes. One person may be reminded, for instance, of his mother singing in the kitchen wearing a blue apron, but there will also be an evocation of the more fundamental energies of blue that come from its integral association with the sky, water, space and coolness. Likewise, red will also always awaken our instinctive response that is connected with the phenomena of heat, blood and life force. We are all generally cheered by reasonably bright colours too, while an excess of drab colours tends to make us feel gloomy.

Carlton Wagner of the Colour Research Institute of Santa Barbara in California has suggested that we have an automatic inherited endo-cranial response to colour, and it is generally accepted that the cells in our body, and not just our visual perception, respond to light and to colour in an unconscious but genetically programmed way. So it is that certain colours and combinations of colours stimulate the most primitive part of our sensory system, the primitive limbic midbrain, which regulates basic body functions such as temperature, hunger and libido, and evokes the kind of response that we needed in ancient times to survive – anger, aggression, and the instinct to fight or take flight, or take protective action. This is still enhanced, in certain situations, by the production of adrenaline when we see red, orange and yellow light, and when these colours are combined with black, as in the common patterns found in dangerous animals and insects mentioned above. These associations still live on in our deeper unconscious, and so are part of the effects of these colours in relevant circumstances. More subtle distinctions of colour, which we have gradually evolved since these times, are processed by the cerebral cortex – the outer portion of the

brain which has developed more recently, and which controls humanity's higher functions.

Ancient humankind also developed associations with colours that involved other important emotional phenomena – sexuality, power, happiness, joy and peace, as well as aggression and danger. The associated colours became more and more deeply entrenched in our psychological make-up, and are still operative today, perhaps all the more important as we may not be directly aware of them. However, it is generally held that we are slowly moving as a species from a predominantly red-based awareness, involving underlying signals of warning and danger, to a more blue-based system of perception, which is more responsive to the concepts of relaxation, ease and beauty. We have evolved from being totally preoccupied with the experiences of hunting and foraging for food and defending ourselves from wild beasts to having progressively easier lives with increasing opportunity for leisure, artistic and creative expression and the pursuit of pleasure. This, of course, is an extremely lengthy process! Interestingly, though, those early danger-signal colour combinations, notably red and black or yellow and black, have become extremely popular in fashion. Could it be that in cases such as these there is an unconscious desire in the wearers to let people know that they may be angry, volatile or dangerous, and that others should keep their distance or avoid intimate contact?

THE SCIENCE OF COLOUR

Scientific knowledge confirms the means by which these powerful effects occur. Colour is something that we respond to from the depths of our psyche. The retina of the eye is the largest of all users of the brain's neurones, occupying over 30 per cent of the capacity of the cortex of the brain, compared with only 3 per cent used for hearing, for instance.

Whenever we see light or colour there is a biochemical transformation within our body cells, via hormones that have a profound effect on our moods and emotions, our physical well-being and our behaviour. For instance, colour entering the optical system can stimulate the production of melatonin, a hormone secreted by the pineal gland, which is located inside the top of the skull; this regulates our sleep patterns and mood swings, and determines whether we feel drowsy or alert. Colour also stimulates or depresses the hypothalamus gland, which in turn directly affects the pituitary gland. This latter is the master gland which controls the whole hormonal system, including the sex glands. Thus, perceived colour has an effect on all hormonal secretions into the bloodstream.

Humankind is not slow to make use of this type of response to colour, starting with the basic distinction that red stimulates tension and excitement, while blue can lessen anxiety and hostility and increase our sense of relaxation. It has been known for some time, for instance, that the colour orange stimulates the appetite; thus this colour is often used in fast food chains and in advertising, to manipulate a hunger response. Blue, on the other hand, is an appetite depressant, and so could be helpful to people who want to lose weight! The hot colours – red, orange and yellow – are often used in advertising, clothing and decor to create an impression of vitality and liveliness, while blues, greens and violets are often employed to create a sense of calmness, serenity and freedom. In an influential marketing experiment run by advertising experts, a packet of identical washing detergent was offered in three different packaging colourings – one yellow, one blue and one a mixture of the two. The researchers found that, for the majority of people, the two-colour carton was most appealing because the actual powder in the yellow carton was considered too powerful and that in the blue one too weak. The middle powder was 'just right'!

Blue walls have been used in mental hospitals to keep patients calmer; if the same colour is used on the walls of a cafeteria, however, employees complain of the cold. A clinical psychologist by the name of Alexander Schauss developed a soft shade of pink which has been used widely to paint prison walls and is said to have dramatically reduced stress and violent behaviour among inmates. In educational buildings, some shades of yellow have been found to enable faster learning in the classroom, while others induce nausea!

In fact, there is a whole new occupation – colour consultancy – which specializes in applying these principles on behalf of clients, especially in large-scale commerce and industry, where measurable productivity is at a premium and anything that will enhance it is eagerly embraced and paid for handsomely. Colour management principles are applied to spaces according to the purpose and activities they house – factories, offices and hospitals will all have very different requirements. Consultants even offer advice on matters such as how to make trains more visible at level crossings – all using essentially the same principles as are used in colour healing.

Many of these effects have been quantified this century. In the 1930s a psychologist named Kurt Goldstein discovered that the colour red in a person's environment caused him or her to over-estimate time. He also found that red objects appeared larger, heavier and longer than those coloured blue or green. A study of dock workers experimented with different colourings of the crates that the men were lifting; when these were black, there were many complaints about the weight, but crates of the same weight painted green appeared to be no problem at all to lift.

Professor Max Luscher developed a still celebrated system of colour analysis, the Luscher Colour Test, for assessing patients' psychological and physiological characteristics according to which colours they like or dislike. This is widely thought to reveal such significant information as whether a patient is insecure, aggressive, trustworthy, emotionally stable, compulsively overworking, or at risk from heart attack – or possibly even at the end of his or her tether, and likely to commit suicide.

Dr Seymour Fisher, professor of psychiatry at the State University of New York, points up the use of similar principles:

> If you feel too open to intrusion, or that your body is fragile, wearing bright colours may be a way of protecting yourself.

Here is a summary of the accepted psychological meanings and effects of the main colours:

Dark Blue	Confident
	Conservative
	Responsible
	Reliable
	Tranquil
	Introspective
	Discerning
	Intuitive
	Intelligent
	Wise
Light Blue	Peaceful
	Loving
	Affectionate
	Idealistic
	Communicative

	Sincere
	Creative
	Possessing will-power

Blue-Green	Sophisticated
	Creative
	Egocentric
	Fussy
	Orderly

Green	Peaceful
	Loyal
	Balanced
	Generous
	Stable
	Sensitive
	Endearing
	Tenacious

Yellow-Green	Perceptive
	Non-judgemental
	Fearful

Yellow	Cheerful
	Enthusiastic
	Intelligent
	Powerful
	Optimistic
	Competitive
	Variable

White	Neat
	Orderly
	Critical
	Self-sufficient
	Cautious

	Motivated
	Spiritual
	Positive
Grey	Tranquil
	Aloof
	Guarded
Black	Sophisticated
	Serious
	Authoritative
	Dramatic
	Dignified
	Secure
	Mystifying
	Death
	The unknown
Beige	Well-adjusted
	Balanced
	Hardworking
	Reliable
	Honest
Brown	Passive
	Receptive
	Loyal
	Homespun
	Sense of duty
	Hardworking
	Toiling/drudgery
Orange	Warm
	Creative
	Joyful
	Immediate

Assertive
Expressive
Sexual

Pink   Loving
Relaxed
Warm-hearted
Maternal

Red   Energetic
Sensual
Successful
Impulsive
Restless
Extroverted
Impatient
Intense

Purple   Spiritual
Sensitive
Intuitive
Open-minded
Welcoming

Violet   Intricate
Mystical
Unifying
Enchanting

PHYSICAL EFFECTS OF COLOUR

Much of the above description of the psychological effects of colour carries implications for its physical effects as well, especially in terms of the effects of the stimulation of adrenaline and other hormones. However, there are many other ways that colour affects us in terms of our physical health.

Again, it has been in this century that traditional knowledge about specific effects has been quantified and affirmed by modern technological methods. In 1924 the Russian scientist Krakow carried out extensive tests, and confirmed that the colour red stimulated particularly the sympathetic portion of the autonomous nervous system, and therefore all the functions that it controls, while blue stimulates the parasympathetic portion of that system. In the 1950s, Dr Harry Wohlfach used the autonomous nervous system as a reaction indicator, to demonstrate that particular colours have consistent, predictable and measurable effects. For instance, he verified that the collective metabolic system of blood pressure, pulse rate and rate of respiration is decreased slightly by the effects of green, decreased more by blue, and most of all by black. The same system, he found, is increased a little by red, more by orange and most of all by yellow.

Light as a composite entity has long been known to have a dramatic effect on human well-being, but modern science has shown just how it is that the effects take place. A disrupted supply of natural light such as is experienced during travel or in winter in northern latitudes, for instance, alters the subtle interplay of a great variety of brain chemicals; this produces dramatic effects, such as interruption of sleep patterns, depression, jet lag and the now much-publicized Seasonal Affective Disorder. It has become clear from these and other studies that the ancients were right – we are not only affected by colour through seeing it; our actual body cells are light-sensitive. Even our organs are sensitive to changes between day and night and directly affected by light and colour, because the human body is actually quite translucent. So when we decide what colour of clothing to

26   wear, we are actually choosing coloured filters with which to give our body a colour treatment that day! The effects of colour on physical ailments and our well-being in general will be dealt with in much more detail in Chapter 4 (where the emphasis will be on using many different practical methods of colour healing).

HOW COLOUR HEALING IS PRACTISED

et's now look at the many different ways that colour healing is put into practice today. There are a number of different 'schools of thought' among those who use colour healing as a complementary health therapy, some more esoteric than others. Colour healing is also used in the field of conventional health care around the world.

Let's first learn a little about each of the prominent figures who have put modern colour healing on the map as a respectable alternative or complementary therapy. These are pioneering figures, most of whom have dedicated their lives to these studies and who have probably all been thought mad or eccentric when they first started out on their careers. Most of these schools of thought now have considerable numbers of adherents, some of whom are respected practitioners, who offer reputable programmes of workshops for those who have an interest or who want full training. (Information on how to contact these resources is contained in the Appendix.)

Ghadiali was a Hindu scientist who worked in the US around the 1930s; his research and theories form the basis of much of modern colour therapy, or chromotherapy as he called it. He showed scientifically that colours are actually *potent chemical entities* which operate as vibrations of high frequency. He articulated the effects of these colour vibrations on all organisms, including the human body, so that for each functional system there would be a particular colour which enhanced the operation of that system, and another that suppressed it. This information, he proved, makes it possible to bring in the right colour that is needed to correct the functioning of any of the organ systems that has gone wrong. Ghadiali articulated the proper inter-balance of colour energies in the whole person, in order to reduce or avoid disease and to increase all aspects of well-being.

Ghadiali further verified what all the ancient sciences already agreed upon – that the functioning of the human aura (or energy envelope) is crucial to this whole process. He argued that all life on our planet obtains its energy from the sun's radiation, consisting of white or natural sunlight, which charges the earth's atmosphere with energy and creates all the chemical interactions that take place on earth. The aura, or charged energy field around human beings, absorbs light from the sun and processes it as a variety of individual colour components, which then vitalize all the different functions of the physical body. (The aura is described in more detail in Chapter 4.)

Looking into this process further, Ghadiali analysed the effects of individual colour rays on particular parts of human metabolism, which he defined as a dynamic balance between the opposing elements of *anabolism*, that is, construction and repairing functions, and *catabolism*, or the breaking down and

removal of unwanted materials such as toxins. He realized that red is the chief colour of anabolism, stimulating, for instance, the liver and the production of red blood cells. At the other end of the visible spectrum, violet stimulates the spleen, which removes unwanted red blood cells and creates white blood cells, a major component in fighting infection. Midway between these ends of the spectrum is the colour green, which stimulates the pituitary gland, enabling a balancing function to be carried out by all the other glands which are controlled by it. This is why green is a very powerful balancing colour. Ghadiali considered, as mentioned in Chapter 2, that the primary colours should be those of the visible spectrum – red, green and violet.

Ghadiali argued that chromotherapy was far preferable to the increasing reliance on drugs that occurred in his time, because the components of natural light matched the chemicals of which the human organism is composed, whereas drugs are foreign bodies. Mary Anderson quotes him as saying that 'To endeavour to introduce haphazard inorganic metals into an organic machine is like feeding a baby with steel tacks to make it strong'! Chromotherapy, unlike drug treatment, does not leave residues that need to be eliminated by the body, and it works at the causative rather than symptomatic level of ill-health.

Mary Anderson, author of *Colour Therapy* (first published in 1975), is one of the many leading colour therapists who have based their work on Ghadiali's theories, with an emphasis on the importance of the aura, chakras and subtle body, and on the use of the seven major colour rays.

THEO GIMBEL

Theo Gimbel is one of the most significant figures in this field. Although his work tends to seem extremely esoteric, it has been

very influential; many of today's leading authors on the subject began as his pupils.

Theo Gimbel is from Germany. His own passion for the world of colour began with a spell of three and a half years as a prisoner of war in Russia, where he was often kept in complete darkness. He decided that the senses are the gateway to healing, and that the eyes and colour were probably the most powerful of these because colour is more ethereal than other vibrations, and so affects the human aura and other subtle energy fields most strongly. It operates at high frequencies, and so can heal conditions caused by the finest imbalances in the body. To him, colour is the doorway which leads deep into the mind. He has been well aware that the whole body is light-sensitive, allowing colour to be absorbed through its cell structure as well as through the eyes. It is Gimbel's opinion that all matter, even inanimate objects, has an electromagnetic energy field and therefore an aura of colour – the denser the matter, the brighter the colours. He believes that colour healing was used in Atlantis, and down through human history ever since.

Gimbel's work has been strongly influenced by Goethe's theory of colour, and on how this was developed and applied by Rudolf Steiner, the founder of Anthroposophy, which places strong emphasis on the importance of spirituality in all kinds of human activity, from education to making furniture. Gimbel established the Hygeia School of Colour many years ago, and he continues to carry out research there into the healing effects of colour and the interacting principles of colour, form, sound and movement; and also to teach what he has discovered there. These courses are attended by lay people, medical people and educationalists. Gimbel also designs colour schemes and interiors for hospitals, schools and clinics, according to individual needs and problems. His Studios design and market equipment for individual and commercial use, such as coloured silks and lamps with variable colour filters.

Gimbel has developed a number of distinctive areas of specialization in his work with colour. One of the most interesting concerns the relevance of colour to the spine, upon which he places great emphasis as the balancing factor of the body. He divides the spinal chord into five octaves of eight colours as they appear in the rainbow spectrum. These octaves also correspond to notes on the musical scale, each of which will then have a healing effect on the corresponding vertebrae. Dowsing is first used to determine which of a patient's vertebrae are injured or misaligned, and then the appropriate colour is administered with coloured light. A music therapist takes the notes corresponding to the affected vertebrae and makes a musical composition from them, which can then be recorded for the patient.

Gimbel has also done much work with the use of crystals, and has evolved a set of archetypal geometrical shapes or patterns which are used in conjunction with the healing colours. He is concerned, too, with the effect of light and colour on the unconscious mind and on our cellular memory. He believes that in order properly to heal the predicament in which humankind finds itself today, it is necessary to look back at our origins, to go right back to the origins of matter and the stages through which our planet and life developed: namely, first darkness, then light, then colour and sound, and then form. Much of his understanding of how colour works and how it affects us draws on this kind of analysis.

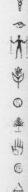

AURA SOMA

Aura Soma originated years ago when a woman named Vicky Wall developed a series of coloured oil-based essences. She became blind because of a stroke, and in her late sixties developed this method of colour healing intuitively. These coloured fluids are a mixture of cosmetic oils, herbal potions and aromatherapy essences, each with its own distinctive colour, contained in clear glass bottles; the mixture may also include either one or two separate, non-mixing colours. *Aura*, as we have seen, is the subtle electro-magnetic energy field around the body, and *Soma* means the being who resides in that body. The highly coloured appearance of up to a hundred of these jewel-like containers is a distinctive feature of Aura Soma. Vicky died before she had fully explored the potential of this tool, but her work has been carried on by the Aura Soma organization, which gives readings and treatments to clients, and trains new practitioners.

The essences are used in a variety of ways. First of all, they can be used for a colour reading, where a client is encouraged to use intuition to choose the four bottles that he or she is attracted to from among the whole range, to create a sense of balance. The first bottle is chosen to represent the aura and the past, representing the evolutionary development of the person's spirit. The second and third bottles represent the person's present development of this life, and his or her life purpose. The fourth bottle chosen is regarded as representing the present and future. The practitioner relates all these choices together, then deduces information about the client's health and well-being, including emotional and psychic matters, as much from what has *not* been chosen as from what *has*. It is claimed that even information about healing made necessary as a result of past life incarnations may be gathered in this way.

The coloured essences are then used, singly or in combinations, for the actual healing. The client may be given bottles that are made up to match the chosen colours and essences. These can then be applied to the skin, or used visually, according to the client's preference and the condition involved. Some people use them in structured meditation, others have them around the home to look at when needed. This is thought to awaken the individual's connection with the world of colour, and to develop one's intuitive ability to use colour, instead of relying on another person's judgement.

So Aura Soma is thought to regenerate, revitalize and rebalance the human aura, not just to treat symptoms but also to replenish the energies of the colour components that are weakened. It is claimed that a great variety of complaints can be helped in these ways, and that numerous remarkable and spontaneous healings have taken place thus. Naturally, the degree of success will depend to a considerable extent on the diagnostic and interpretative skill and experience of the practitioner who initiates the process. The profundity of the method is based on the conviction that our relationship with colours is the reflection of our soul, and that we all have an instinct to know which aspect of our spirit may be in need of healing and to identify and absorb the precise colours we need. So the essences are able to heal wounded or fragmented parts of the psyche as well as physical ills, including imbalances in the chakra system and the aura.

ALICE HOWARD

Alice Howard has been an influence in this field for many decades, combining colour work with homoeopathy, biochemistry and other healing methods. Alice has worked with colour therapy as a form of distant healing, when the patient is not present, using a pendulum to make a diagnosis. She has

emphasized that physical treatment is not the most vital component in dealing with illness; it is often essential for dealing with underlying habits of behaviour and thought that are part of the cause, and which may be buried deep in the subconscious.

PAULINE WILLS

Pauline Wills combines colour healing with foot reflexology, rebalancing the energies of the whole body by applying colour to specific points on the feet. This can often be used where the patient's condition is extremely weak or delicate, or where direct intervention such as conventional reflexology pressure would otherwise be inadvisable. Boxes lined with mirrors are slipped over the feet, permitting the radiation of coloured light onto the soles.

MARIE LOUISE LACEY

Marie Louise Lacey is author of *Know yourself through Colour*, which includes a pack of colour cards that can be used for readings on health and life in general.

HOWARD SUN

Howard Sun works with personality types through colour, first doing an analysis and then applying appropriate colour radiation using a crystal. His emphasis is on how colour raises awareness and transforms consciousness.

LILY CORNFORD

Lily, of the Matraya School of Healing, is one example of the many healers who use colour to some extent in their work, for instance as an additional method of shifting energy blockages in the body or auric field. Advice on colours that the patient may then continue to use, such as in clothing, is often also

given. Lily teaches practitioners to heal by projecting colours
from their own chakras, through visualization.

THE ATLANTEANS

Followers of this occult movement believe that the peoples of
the ancient culture of Atlantis used colour healing in very profound and powerful ways, which can still be accessed by developing one's mental powers and visualization. Practitioners
direct colours through their hands to their patients.

AMBIKA WAUTERS

Ambika has created homoeopathic colour remedies. She uses
these for healing physical pathology as well as emotional and
mental imbalance.

Further exploration of many of these concepts, together with
guidance on how to use similar methods yourself, will be
found in the following chapter.

COLOUR HEALING IN
CONVENTIONAL HEALTH CARE

Colour healing is not only an alternative or complementary
therapy; increasingly it is used routinely as part and parcel of
modern medical care, often in a context of highly sophisticated and automated technology. Such uses, in fact, go back to
the earliest historical examples of what we think of as modern
Western allopathic medicine (*see Chapter 1*).

A great deal of medically-orientated laboratory research
over the years, especially during this century, has validated
the effects and qualities of colour and light, and formed the
basis for increasing the possible uses of this type of healing.
Tests have ranged from experiments on the effect of different

types of light on plant growth, to showing how abnormal cell functioning in humans could have been caused by losing the effect of key components in natural light. As early as 1926, the new science of chromotherapy had moved to a point where Dr Kate Baldwin, a senior surgeon for 23 years at Philadelphia Women's Hospital in the US, was able to say, 'I can produce quicker and more accurate results with colour than with all other methods combined.'

Chromotherapy and related methods are now regularly used in a wide variety of ways in modern hospitals. Operating theatres use ultra-violet (UV) light, an astringent and anti-bacterial agent, to cleanse walls, tables and instruments after operations, as indeed UV is used increasingly throughout the food industry to destroy bacteria and prevent fungal growth.

The main branch of chromotherapy is in the prescribing of specific coloured light to deal with a variety of ailments. An early study by Dr Sharon McDonald at the State University School of Nursing at San Diego substantiated traditional awareness that blue light is capable of soothing inflammation and reducing the effects of high blood pressure; this knowledge has since passed into common usage. Blue light is also widely used to reduce the pain of inflammatory arthritis. Blue is used, too, to treat premature babies, whose livers are usually underdeveloped so they cannot transform the chemical bilirubin which accumulates under the skin and which can cause brain damage or even death. Blue light breaks down this substance in about three days, by which time the liver is usually sufficiently mature to function unaided.

Red light is specifically effective, for instance, in the treatment of poor circulation and stiff joints, and of non-inflammatory rheumatism and arthritis. It has also been found to be extremely effective in the symptomatic treatment of migraine.

Red and blue light have both proven useful in improving the physical performance of the human body; this knowledge has been exploited in specialized fields such as athletics. Looking at red increases strength by up to 5 or 6 per cent, providing the extra performance needed in sudden bursts of action by increasing electrical activity in the muscles of the arms and legs. Looking at blue, on the other hand, enhances the steady flow of energy output over longer periods.

More and more advanced applications of colour are constantly being developed in medicine today, and new colour-related sciences invented: one example is the specialized field of PhotoDynamic Therapy, or PDT. Dr T. Dougherty of Buffalo, New York, found that certain chemicals which are photosensitive, or sensitive to the effects of light, tend to accumulate in cancer cells in the body after being intravenously injected into the system. Not only that, but once they have accumulated at such cancer sites, they can be picked up and located under ultra-violet light. When activated by infra-red light (which is able to penetrate the body deeply due to its extremely large wavelength), the cancerous cells can then be specifically and exclusively destroyed using fibre optics, without affecting surrounding healthy tissue.

As well as being used in medical treatment, colour is widely employed in a variety of diagnostic applications, to identify the nature of illness. Most straightforwardly, the colour of the skin, tongue, eyes and various bodily secretions are very well-established indicators of one's state of health. Purple or blue skin, for instance, is a sign of lack of oxygen in the blood, and is often associated with heart disease. More advanced applications include Infra-red Thermography, where minute but significant temperature differences are detected and picked up as colour variations, thus pinpointing a variety of problems including blood clots or cancerous tumours.

Interesting crossovers have been occurring in the ways of diagnosing illness between the approaches of alternative health, drawing on traditional wisdom, and modern science. This is particular true of work concerning the human aura, that field of subtle electro-magnetic energy which surrounds the body and extends about 45 – 60 cm outwards from it, roughly oval in shape and often referred to as 'a faint, luminous mist'. Before the First World War, Dr W. J. Kilner, a medical electrician at St Thomas Hospital in London, created a device which came to be known as the Kilner screen. Dr Kilner was convinced that imminent ill-health shows up in the aura earlier and more graphically than in manifest physical symptoms. So he set about creating an instrument that could detect the patterns and changes in the auric field.

The device which he came up with consists of two glass plates, and between them is a solution of diayinin, a dye that is indigo to violet in colour. This renders the aura more visible, as most people cannot see it unaided or without special training. Colours which then become visible within the auric field are then interpreted by a trained observer. Colour component 'deficiencies' are then detected, along similar lines of interpretation as are used in conventional colour healing – with red and orange representing effects associated with heat and activity (as when a patient is over-stressed), blue to violet indicating effects to do with cooling and passivity (as when a patient is lacking in energy), and green as the representative of balance or harmony. Appropriate light treatment can then be prescribed, by whatever means preferred.

However, Dr Kilner's work has not passed into conventional medical usage; perhaps he was just too far ahead of his time. But Kirlian photography is different and more widely accepted today. When it was first discovered in the former USSR during the 1960s, the Soviet academic and medical world immediately began to take interest, and some began to take the human aura seriously for the first time. This took place behind the Iron Curtain, of course, where scientists had been studying human energy fields for some time, probably in the interests of Cold War military supremacy. An operative by the name of Simyon Kirlian (again, an electrician!) found a way of photographing the aura that surrounds both people and other living entities. He photographed plant leaves and vegetables, and it was soon demonstrated that the appearance of the aura was very much a function of changes in the health and life energy of all things. More dramatically, it was then found that these changes could occur three weeks before they would show up in the outward, physical ill-health of the organism!

In 1968, Kirlian photography was demonstrated in conjunction with hands-on healing at a major scientific conference, where it was graphically shown that there was a pronounced difference in the aura pattern after healing had taken place.

SEASONAL AFFECTIVE DISORDER

SAD, or Seasonal Affective Disorder, has become a very well-known phenomenon in recent years; although it has been unofficially recognized for probably much longer, it was during the 1970s and 1980s that breakthroughs were made in its scientific investigation. In 1981, Dr Norman Rosenthal published some authoritative findings about the condition. Having surveyed the phenomenon across a large number of sample cases and over a long period of time, he identified SAD as a physical and emotional response to seasonally varying light conditions. This occurs particularly during the winter, but in extreme latitudes it can apply to the whole period from late autumn through to spring. People who are vulnerable to the condition can experience loss of energy, the desire to sleep a great deal, increase in appetite and resulting weight gain, loss of interest in sex, and feelings of being withdrawn, gloomy or even depressed. This disorder was found to affect four times as many women as men.

SAD is actually thought to be a result of a residual human tendency to hibernate, a historical reflex stimulated by changing environmental light levels, developed in prehistoric times when hibernation was biologically necessary due to diminished food supplies and exposure to extreme weather conditions. The pineal gland in particular is crucial to this response: it regulates the body's vitality and life force, controls sleep patterns, influences sexuality, prompts the onset of puberty and greatly affects mood; it is the body's light meter.

Falling daylight levels bring about the increased secretion of melatonin (mentioned in Chapter 2). In later research, Drs Leavy and Wehr discovered that by artificially simulating the effects of a longer winter day on patients, excessive melatonin production was suppressed, and the SAD symptoms radically reduced. It was also discovered that full-spectrum lighting (FSL) worked significantly better in this regard than other forms of artificial light. Further research has led to still more effective refinement of techniques: lights of five times the standard brightness are now used, and have been found to be most effective when applied in the morning. Furthermore, light from the red end of the spectrum works best of all.

What all these techniques do, essentially, is to trick the body into thinking that it's spring when it's actually winter, so that the glandular system responds accordingly. It is interesting to note, though, that the many people not affected by

SAD may be generally healthier, or may be consciously or unconsciously taking other measures that enable their system to adapt successfully to prevailing light conditions, such as by altering their activities and lifestyle. Before the Industrial Revolution, people were obliged to live lives that were necessarily governed by environmental conditions, including light levels. So in winter people were less busy and worked less hard because it was a less busy agricultural time, they stayed in more and slept longer; they didn't have electric lighting – and they may well have been happy to put on weight in order to cope with the cold, without central heating. By contrast, our patterns of modern living generally demand a constant level of comfort conditions, patterns of activity and productivity, so the primitive body response becomes a problem where it wasn't before.

It's also revealing that women are more affected by SAD than men. Studies have also shown that light affects other aspects of female sexuality and reproduction, again especially in extreme latitudes. In *Colour and Human Responses*, Faber Brinnen reports that with Inuit and Eskimo women increased melatonin production can cause ovulation and menstruation to cease completely during the long, dark winter months. More interestingly still, this coincides with a dramatic decrease in libido and sperm production in men! Even in temperate latitudes there is a noticeable element of this effect – hence the popular metaphors about spring and 'rising sap', and so on. The Eskimos and other peoples have managed to evolve – or perhaps to preserve – a natural form of birth control which ensures that children are conceived at the right time of year to be born in the warmer months, when they will have a much better chance of surviving the crucial early months of life.

Starting from awareness of these phenomena, medical science has evolved ways of dealing with reproductive problems.

The pineal gland affects the whole of our sexual psychology, and phototherapy can now be used to treat a wide variety of sexual dysfunction. PMS, too, can be treated in this way; exposing patients to bright light in the evening for a week prior to the onset of menstruation has been shown to prevent PMS completely.

Other problems that are akin to SAD are also helped by light treatment. So simulated light therapy is now used for shift workers, poor sleepers, frequent flyers and other people who are affected by altered shifts in their daily cycle. These benefits have all been found to be particularly enhanced when the light used is full-spectrum; studies of normal fluorescent lighting in particular have shown that it is not only lacking in important colour components, but is actively harmful. It is deficient at the blue end of the spectrum, releasing chiefly red, yellow and orange light, and creating a distorted spectrum effect. Studies carried out by Dr Fritz Hollwich in 1980 showed that people who work under these lights for long periods develop high blood levels of the hormones ACTH and cortisol; in excess, these hormones produce a stress response. Full-spectrum artificial lighting does not produce this effect.

Full-spectrum lighting (FSL) can also play an important part in helping with child behaviour in schools. Dr John Ott, an American pioneer in the development of light medicine, found that an environment of FSL calms down children who are hyperactive, and enhances the capabilities of children who have reading and learning disabilities. In fact, compared with other forms of artificial lighting, FSL has been shown to enhance almost all aspects of human well-being.

Finally, we can briefly mention the field of human psychology and mental health, where great strides are again being made in the medical use of light and colour. Hospitals for the mentally ill now choose colour schemes with particular attention to their effects on patients. Mary Anderson describes one example, a room set up for particularly disturbed patients at Worcester State Hospital in Massachusetts. This is known as 'the green room': it has light green walls, large green bathtubs, and green window shades with light filtering through in a way that gives something of the atmosphere of an undersea cave. In other parts of the same hospital there are light green beds, with walls of pale green, grey or yellow, which altogether have been found to create a tranquil atmosphere and a calming effect on agitated patients.

Psychologists are now able to draw up highly elaborate and accurate personality profiles and character analyses from detailed tests based on colour preferences and choices. These tests have been developed and used over the last 60 years, originating with the work of Luscher, who pioneered work with the concept that one's colour preferences show much about one's state of mind. He proved that when we see a colour there is always a personal reaction; he then devised the first tests that reveal information about a person's psychological make-up. He concluded, for instance, that a preference for green can indicate that a person may dislike change, for violet, a reliance on others, and for black, stubbornness. He also showed that use of corresponding colours can help with resolving personality and psychological issues revealed in this way.

Not only clinical psychology but also business and industry have been quick to take these findings on board. Corresponding tests are used extensively to determine the suitability

of applicants for a new job, a transfer or promotion. The same awareness of colour has also proved invaluable in choosing office and factory environments which will be most productive, efficient and harmonious.

THE TWO STRANDS OF HEALING

It is interesting to note some broad differences between colour healing as a complete system, albeit alternative or complementary, and as a component of modern scientific medicine and technology. Apart from the obvious differences that arise from differing goals and philosophical positions, such as how holistic the respective methods are, and whether the treatment involved is symptomatic or able to work at a causative level, there are also differences in the basic approach to colour. One of the most significant is that colour healing as a complementary therapy almost exclusively draws on the naturally occurring colours of the visible spectrum (*see page 15*), whereas technological health care, as we have seen above, focuses particularly on the extremes of light, such as ultra-violet and infra-red, which must be artificially synthesized and whose incidental effects may not be fully understood for many years. This means a departure from the 'natural' approach which many specialists feel is safer, more appropriate and more effective than synthesizing new forces that do not exist in nature.

It can be argued that allopathic medicine proceeds more slowly than its more radical counterpart, needing everything to be proved scientifically and then having to discover a technological method to put into practice what has been observed before it can become part of mainstream care. It is also argued that colour healing, as a therapy in itself, develops pragmatically and draws upon the wisdom of the ancients, thus avoiding the constant effort that could be spent on reinventing the wheel; it develops in leaps and bounds that are made possible by the work of a limited number of individual visionaries. None the less, as time passes modern allopathic medicine is increasingly influenced by both alternative and traditionally-based health disciplines such as acupuncture and even spiritual healing, and it seems clear that a merging of these two overall approaches to the use of colour is taking place, especially in Europe and the US.

METHODS YOU CAN
USE YOURSELF

I n this chapter, we will show you how to apply – practically, in your own home and in everyday life – what you have discovered so far about the immense potential of colour healing. These methods are simple and easy to use. You might be concerned with boosting your energy levels. You might wish to recover from stress, or to prevent it occurring. You might be suffering from a particular physical illness. You might be suffering emotionally, or in spirit. Colour healing brings many possibilities: it works at all levels, to heal and regenerate the mind, body and spirit, for it is able to transform all kinds of energy imbalances. So when you use it, changes may take place at all levels, even if you started out thinking only about your most immediate needs. Changes can take place in both obvious, tangible ways and in more subtle, less immediately perceptible ones; you may well find that using these methods can lead you to a more profound understanding of yourself and of your deeper nature – especially if you are open to such possibilities. As it naturally rebalances the energy field of your body, it can also move you to a new level of awareness.

Some people are attracted to begin to use colour consciously when they are undergoing deep physical, emotional or psychological changes, when they are intuitively drawn to the stabilizing influence that it can provide. During the authors' own lives, there have been numerous times of change and turmoil when work with colour has given a very strong and positive anchoring influence. The same applies to many of our friends and clients.

One such woman was going through extreme trauma due to a painful divorce, in which her ex-partner was handling things extremely unpleasantly; she was suffering physically, emotionally and materially. She was advised simply to wear green as often as possible, and she did so; as we have learned, green is frequently used for balance and peace, and has a strong neutralizing influence. This woman was soon re-experiencing a sense of stability in her life, and from this position she was able to make the transition successfully from being part of a broken couple to being a happy single person.

Indeed, we often see that people who are going through changes and adjustments in life are actually able to absorb unconsciously the influence of the very colours that they need for the situation and the emotions in question. So just as the woman just mentioned could feel, as soon as it was recommended to her, the rightness of green as the influence that could anchor her heart energy and give her broken heart a sense of mending, so others are attracted to what is appropriate for them. Perhaps it will be yellow, the colour that we need when we must get in touch with our personal power and awaken our inner spiritual strength. Or maybe it will be magenta, which enables us to make mental and spiritual shifts in our thinking. Or it might be red, which is great when we are too high off the ground and need some good, solid earthing. Whatever our situation, working in these ways with colour will naturally help to awaken or further develop that natural instinct and intuitive ability for healing with

48   colour that we all have, but which may have long been buried below our immediate consciousness.

Some of the techniques offered here are very ancient and have come down to us from millennia of refinement and wise use. Others are very innovative and have become possible because of other developments which are part of the forward progress of humanity. Yet others combine ideas from both these sources. When we draw upon all these sources and adapt them to our particular needs, we can create a unique and powerful tool for our own personal healing.

First we will look at the more practical and physically-orientated methods of using colour and light in healing – working with carefully selected coloured lights, choosing food for its correcting colour influence, and drinking specially coloured fluids. We will also review the full range of colours used in healing, and summarize their qualities and effects as a guide to which you can make reference again and again, once you are familiar with the particular techniques. Then we will go on to examine what we may call 'inner' methods, such as using colour in meditation and visualization.

But before any of this, it is helpful to look again at a phenomenon through which all these methods work: the energy field that surrounds the body and through which all colour that reaches us is filtered – the human aura.

THE AURA AND COLOUR HEALING

As we have read in Chapter 2, modern physics is discovering what many religions and traditional sciences have understood for thousands of years – that everything in the universe is in a sense composed of energy that vibrates at different rates of frequency, so that some of it seems more etheric and some more solid. So light and the colour that it possesses is one example of this kind of energy, and we are another. Then, in Chapter 3, we learned that Kirlian photography has been able to make visible records of an electro-magnetic field that surrounds the body, making a kind of boundary between the body and its surroundings. This is known as the *aura* or *auric field*.

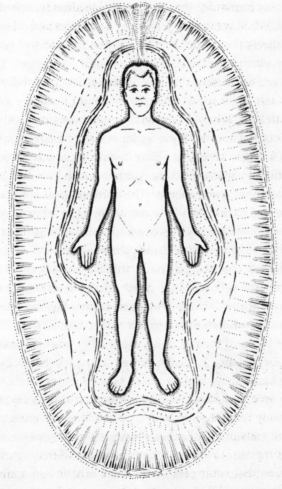

THE AURA

Down through the ages, clairvoyants and other people who have been trained by spiritual methods have been able to see this aura, and it has been often portrayed in pictorial art as 'halos'. Many aspects of this traditional graphic depiction, in fact, are echoed by the way the aura is beginning to be detected by modern technological means, such as Kirlian photography. It has been traditionally thought, and is now scientifically recognized, that the energetic state and inherent colour of the aura reflects the condition of the individual who possesses it, and can change a great deal as that condition changes. This has been verified in terms of the representation of the physical health and life force of a person, animal or plant. At a more sophisticated level, traditional wisdom associates certain colours of the aura with particular stages of a person's spiritual development, and these have been consistently represented in painting by many different cultures which have had no communication with one another. The auras of great spiritual masters are said to radiate all the colours in a luminous way, merging into white. Other beings of a high spiritual state are thought to radiate versions of the three primary colours in their auras, with the red appearing as pink, which is the colour of universal love, and yellow transformed into gold around the head, which we are all familiar with from many religious images.

Other colour manifestations are said to be able to indicate the state of being of the rest of us, especially our emotional states. Black, for instance, indicates hatred or malice, while flashes of red on black show violent anger. Grey denotes fear. Ordinary yellow around the head implies strong dependence on intellect. Depression is visible as blue or black lines of energy at the edges of the aura. And a miser is supposed to have brown lines around the aura! Authorities generally agree that in a healthy, happy and balanced person, the colours of the aura are bright and full of energy, whereas if one is unwell they are generally dull; as Mary Louise Lacey points out, we unconsciously acknowledge this when we say we are feeling 'washed out' or 'off colour'. She also argues that people may well be widely able, albeit unconsciously or intuitively, to pick up on the aura of another person and understand what is going on with him or her without any other evidence, as when we walk into a room and immediately pick up on anger or some other 'atmosphere', or when we sense that someone feels vulnerable.

As well as serving as an indicator, the aura also acts as a kind of protection for our personal energy field; when the aura is 'damaged' we are vulnerable to illness and loss of vital life force. The phenomenon of the 'energy vampire' – the sort of person we all know at least one example of, who makes others feel exhausted when they're with them – is often considered to be experiencing a kind of 'leaking' of life energy from the auric field, which is then replenished at the expense of others.

Whether you would go as far as accepting this kind of explanation, it is none the less clear that this energy field around the body is crucial as an agency in the process by which light and colour affect our well-being. More reference to this will be made as we refer to particular methods of putting colour healing into practice.

THE CHAKRA SYSTEM

The electro-magnetic energy system that consists of both the auric field and the internal patterns within the body has traditionally been analysed as a series of sub-systems; this analysis is extremely helpful and revealing in terms of understanding how colour affects us and how we can use it to be more well and more happy. And again, there is an extraordinary degree of uniformity in description and analysis of what we know as *the chakra system* across many different cultures and over vast periods of time.

Each of the chakras represents one of the seven layers of the aura, which are known esoterically as the 'seven bodies', ranging from the grossest or most physical aspect of our presence to the more subtle or etheric. The chakra system can thus be seen as a sub-division of the whole energy field of the human body, which enables us to associate discrete colours of the spectrum with each of the body's vertical zones, and identify with each colour a whole set of factors including particular emotions, organs and glands and their respective functions, departments of physical health, levels of human faculty, spiritual development and aspects of personality.

Energy is thought of as entering the human field from the cosmos above and from the earth below, and meeting within the body; the chakras are the series of seven vortex points or power centres where these forces mingle, each producing a distinctive energy pattern. They are aligned vertically through the centre of the body, near the spine.

The word *chakra* was given by the ancient yogis of the Indian sub-continent; it means 'wheel of light' in Sanskrit. They formally identified and codified all the properties of the chakras, including the colour associations of each. Each chakra absorbs its appropriate component of vital life force from its own colour or 'ray'. In a healthy and well-balanced state, there is a proper balance between the levels of vibration of the internal energies of all the chakras, and a natural flow through them; but if some are too weak or too strong, or if there is a blockage in the flow, then there will be a corresponding distortion in our pattern of health, or disharmony at some corresponding level of our being. This will also appear as a lack or over-sufficiency of the corresponding colour energy present in the chakra system, which can then be dealt with by colour healing methods. Thus the chakra system gives us the whole elegant and elaborate set of correspondences between particular colours and particular emotions, organs, glands, states of consciousness and everything else.

53

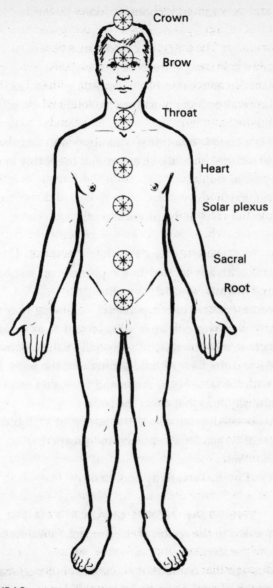

Crown
Brow
Throat
Heart
Solar plexus
Sacral
Root

THE CHAKRAS

off

PRINCIPLES OF COLOUR HEALING

Let's look briefly at each of the chakras and its corresponding colour and governing functions, working upwards.

THE ROOT CHAKRA: RED

This chakra is located at the base of the spine.

It relates to our most basic connection with life and the earth, survival, and the most fundamental and primitive form of our life force.

The associated emotional qualities and attributes are patience, security, stability, structure and the ability to manifest our dreams in reality.

Element: Earth
Purpose: Survival in the physical world

THE SACRAL CHAKRA: ORANGE

The sacral chakra is located in the pelvic area, just below the navel, and inwards towards the spine.

It is representative of our personal well-being in connection with how well we look after ourselves; it is associated with reproduction, movement, sensuality and vitality. It governs our emotions and the flow of fluid throughout the body. It is also linked with the state of the moon and tides, and indeed all the cycles and rhythms that affect the body.

The associated qualities are the feeling of well-being, pleasure, sexuality, gender acceptance and prosperity.

Element: Water
Purpose: Physical creativity and vitality

THE SOLAR PLEXUS CHAKRA: YELLOW

This is located in the region of the stomach (not the abdomen), just below the sternum.

It is through this centre that we harness our personal power and experience our instinctual nature. It feeds energy to the digestive organs, and governs the lower mental functions.

Its related qualities are self-worth and self-esteem, confidence, power and choice.

Element: Fire

Purpose: Attunement with the environment

THE HEART CHAKRA: GREEN

The heart chakra is located at the level of the heart. It is central among the series of chakras, and likewise the core of the human energy system.

This chakra represents balance and the protection of the innocent and pure energy of the heart. It also governs the higher mind.

The associated qualities are love, friendship, brotherhood and freedom.

Element: Air

Purpose: Living in harmony with others

THE THROAT CHAKRA: BLUE/TURQUOISE

The throat chakra is in the middle of the throat area, back towards the centre line of the neck.

It is the centre of communication and the bridge between the feelings of the heart and the thoughts of the mind. It is the centre of spiritual instincts.

Its associated qualities are the energy of will-power, creativity and personal expression.

Element: None

Purpose: Personal expression and truth

THE BROW CHAKRA: INDIGO

This chakra is located directly between the eyebrows.

It stimulates the senses and is associated with the pituitary gland, which regulates vital life functions. It is thus known as the control centre of the body and the spirit, and can deeply affect our moods and attitudes. With the crown chakra, this chakra rules the higher aspirations of the soul. It focuses imagination, knowledge, wisdom, discernment and intuition.

Element: None

Purpose: Wisdom out of life's experiences

THE CROWN CHAKRA: VIOLET

This is located right at the top of the skull, just at the point where a line drawn straight up from the centre of the nose would cross another line followed up from the centre of the ears.

The crown chakra stimulates the pineal gland, which regulates our sleep patterns and other aspects of body light-metering, and feeds us information about times, seasons and cycles, as we have seen in Chapter 3. Thus this centre is particularly strongly affected by the patterns of light to which we are exposed. It is also associated with the higher level of human faculty, including our perception of beauty and our spirituality. It is esoterically regarded as our tie to the forces of the cosmos.

Element: None

Purpose: Spirituality

ATTRIBUTES OF THE MAIN HEALING COLOURS

Going on from this, a wide range of correspondences can be drawn up for the seven major colours, or rays, including the conditions that they can be used to treat. The information that follows has been compiled from a consensus of the major authors on the subject.

Colour	Physical effects	Emotional/psychological effects
Red	Supplies the physical body with energy and vitality, especially the restorative body functions. It grounds us in life and helps us survive. Treatment with red promotes body heat and stimulates the circulation and adrenaline production. Helpful for anaemia, low blood pressure and low vitality; congestive headaches, sluggish bowel, low libido; disperses lethargy, inertia and tiredness, as well as chronic colds and chills. (Because it is so active, red is the most powerful of colours and needs to be used with discrimination in healing, and avoided in cases of high blood pressure.) Has an expansive action.	Uplifts, gives confidence, will-power, courage and a readiness to take initiative and overcome depression, fear or worry.
Orange	Controls the spleen, and so can be used to deal with infections and other disorders of that organ,	Can give physical and mental stimulation and a freeing up of energy – lying, as it does, midway

and for kidney infections, and for bronchitis and other lung problems, lower back trouble, period pains, post-partum healing and gallstones. It is useful for stimulating the appetite. Assists in the assimilative, distributive and circulatory body processes. Stimulates procreation and sensuality. (Having a red component, orange too needs to be used somewhat sparingly. It should not be used in cases of high blood pressure.)

between the red ray of the physical and the yellow ray of the intellect. Reduces repression and overcomes inhibitions, broadening the mind and opening it up to new ideas. Induces understanding and tolerance. Increases vitality and helps us to deal with depression. Lifts the spirits, and can also help to provide vitality and the stamina to cope with life when it seems overpowering or unmanageable.

Yellow

An important centre for the whole nervous system and is a good treatment for nervous exhaustion. It also controls the digestive processes; this means that it has an effect on the eliminative functions of the liver and the intestines, so is an excellent purifier of the whole system, and

Well-known for stimulating the intellectual faculties, the logical mind and the ability to reason, yellow is thus assoc-iated with the power of self-control. After white, yellow is closest to full sun-shine in brightness especially the skin. As well as skin troubles, indigestion, constipation and liver trouble, yellow is also helpful for diabetes. It can also be used in case of hernia, rheumatism and arthritis. It is said, too, to be able to help restore calcium imbalance and aid absorption.

and in hue, and so it nearly always has a stimulating effect on our spirits, bringing a harmonious attitude to life, with a sense of balance and optimism.

Green

Green is used for many health matters related to its corresponding organ, the heart, including improper blood pressure. It is also good for ulcers, for alleviating headaches and the symptoms of flu, and for calming the nervous system. It is also widely recommended for the treatment of cancer, an extreme state of imbalance in the cells. Useful in the drainage of tissues. Finally green can be used more generally to purify and detoxify the blood, and tune up or rebalance the whole body.

Green is, of course, the colour of nature and new life, renewal and the freshness and brightness of spring. It is also the colour of balance, at the midway point of the spectrum range. The agent chlorophyll is what gives plant growth its greenness. Many people working in the field of colour believe that the relative lack of green in urban areas is a major factor in the degeneration of the human spirit and the descent into crime and deprivation that can take place in inner city areas. Helpful for emotional and psychological conditions that involve stress, or the repression of emotion; it is likewise appropriate for various specific kinds of fear – the fear of giving, of involvement or of being hurt.

Blue

Has a predominantly contracting, cooling, restricting or reducing effect, in contrast to the generally expanding and stimulating effect of red; it is extremely useful in slowing down processes and steadying the affairs of the body and mind. Antiseptic and astringent; good for treating any kind of infection where there is fever, inflammation or any rise in temperature. This includes most childhood illnesses, such as measles and

Blue is the classic colour for assisting all kinds of self-expression, including problems with speech. It is extremely powerful in restoring a state of peace and quiet where over-excitement, stress or hysteria have been prevailing.

mumps. Blue is also good
for spasms, stings, itches,
headaches, period pains
and for insomnia and the
treatment of shock. Finally,
it can be used for all problems
of the throat, to which it
particularly relates.

Turquoise

Equally important as an
agency of prevention as of
treatment. The properties
of turquoise are akin to
those of blue; it also relates
to the throat, as well as to
the lungs. It too, is anti-
inflammatory, but has the
additional value of increasing
immunity to all kinds of
unwanted or harmful influences,
from colds or flu to HIV and
other serious immuno-
deficiency conditions.

Increases resistance to
emotional influences,
or even other people,
from which one
wishes to protect
oneself.

Indigo

A powerful combination of
the attributes of deep blue
and the influence of red. At
the physical level, indigo is
akin to blue and so is also
useful for cooling, calming
and soothing, lowering blood
pressure and stopping hae-
morrhaging. It is very much

Having its main effect
through the pineal
gland, indigo affects
most powerfully the
nervous, mental and
psychic aspects of our
well-being and our
capabilities. It can
calm anger, rage or

associated with the nervous system and especially with the organs of sight and hearing, which are closely related to the brow chakra, sometimes known as the 'third eye'. So it can be used to treat conditions of the eyes and ears, and also the nose. May be helpful in asthma and dyspepsia. Indigo can create insensitivity to pain, too, and so can have anaesthetic qualities.

hysteria. It is said to be helpful even with serious mental illness, including obsessions and psychosis, as well as dealing with psychic difficulties.

Violet

Can be used in cases of concussion, rheumatism, tumours, kidney and bladder disorders, cerebrospinal inflammation and physical diseases of the nervous system. Has the highest vibration of the seven main rays.

Associated with the pituitary gland and the crown chakra, the centre of spiritual understanding. Violet goes even further than indigo in dealing with mental and psychological disorders. It is especially helpful for people who are by nature extremely highly strung and nervously disposed, or suffering from neuroses, and is often used to deal with the turbu-

lence and fractious-
ness of an extreme
artistic temperament.
It is helpful in build-
ing up confidence,
and is also a power-
ful aid in the devel-
opment of psychic
and spiritual faculties.

| Magenta | Not one of the seven main rays, the colour magenta is none the less useful on occasion as a healing colour. | Used exclusively at a spiritual level, such as aiding in spiritual understanding when really major changes are taking place in life. Magenta is considered capable of enabling the spirit to connect with the universal consciousness. |

These colours are not recommended as a total cure in themselves, but as an additional method to complement other, more
specific treatments recommended by your health practitioner,
to assist in restoring energetic balance and re-establishing your
vital life force. They can help in healing.

PRACTICAL METHODS OF COLOUR HEALING

HEALING WITH COLOURED LIGHTS

Using coloured lights is one of the most straightforward and effective ways of correcting any imbalances that you may wish to address, whether physical or otherwise. One of the advantages of this type of healing is that you can focus the therapeutic effects specifically on a particular part of the body.

Healing lamps can be purchased complete from schools of colour healing (for details, see the Appendix), or you can easily make them up yourself using coloured transparent gels such as are used in theatre spotlights, which are sold in some art supply shops. These come in shades and hues of almost unlimited variety. They can be cut to fit over any lamp you wish to use. This could be a desk lamp, free-standing lamp or other spotlight, but remember that light bulbs generate a lot of heat and there must be some ventilation gap or means for this to escape, or your gel will burn. Small, second-hand theatrical spotlights are excellent for the purpose.

Remember that the stronger the bulb in the lamp, the more intense the resultant treatment will be. It is best to place yourself between 2 and 4 feet (60 cm to 1.2 m) from the source of light, in the case of a domestic lamp. A theatre lamp may be more powerful, in which case you will need to be further away. You can sit facing the lamp, or arrange it overhead so that it projects down onto you as you lie beneath it. You might even wish to install one in your bathroom so that you can bathe your whole body in coloured water; if you do, though, remember that the electric power supply must be outside the bathroom and the lamp must be positioned so that it cannot fall into the bath under *any* circumstances. Use a timer to regulate the length of treatment, which should be in accordance with the table that follows. Wear either white clothing or none at all, so that you absorb exactly the colour you need.

In addition to the colour directly called for by the condition which you are treating, you will also need to use a gel of the opposite or complementary colour, for the shorter period specified. This rebalances your colour energies to complete the treatment. During the treatment, leave any day-to-day preoccupations, worries and anxieties behind; relax and be in as still, peaceful and tranquil a state as possible. You could play soothing music and burn incense if you wish. As well as absorbing the chosen colours physically, let them also pervade your consciousness.

The following figures represent the maximum time, in minutes, that you should expose yourself to given colours. These time limits should definitely *not* be exceeded. Notice that the red end of the spectrum calls for the shortest time, even when used as a balancing complementary colour.

Colour	Time Period (minutes)	Complementary Colour	Time Period (minutes)
Red	7	Blue	3
Orange	10	Indigo	4
Yellow	12	Violet	6
Green	15	Magenta	7
Blue	15	Red	3
Indigo	15	Orange	4
Violet	15	Yellow	6
Magenta	15	Green	7

HEALING WITH COLOUR IN FOODS

Selecting foods for their natural colours is one of the simplest ways to work with colour healing, specially suited to your individual needs and your regular, day-to-day pattern of life, without the need for equipment or paraphernalia of any kind.

The healing and health-giving properties of food is well known, though many people fail to realize that the inherent colour of a food is one of the major ways in which our energies are benefited by it. All food has colour value, which directly affects our energy levels through nurturing the corresponding physical organs and glands, and affecting our subtle energies by stimulating particular chakras, as described above.

When you are ill, find that your energies are low, are stressed, know you have a particular constitutional health weakness or just wish to exercise preventative health care before an illness develops, let colourful foods work away quietly for your health and well-being. If you are inclined to take vitamin supplements, for instance, reflect that these are really the synthesized products of the foods that you really need, and that you can gain all the benefits in a whole and more effective form by taking the right foods. Similarly, you could be unknowingly exacerbating an unwanted condition or ailment by eating a great deal of food that carries a colour that makes the condition worse. Use the following information as an introduction to this intriguing world of delicious possibilities. Remember that the colour of a plant food that grows above the ground is often in the skin, created there by the life-giving action of sunlight, and so wherever possible it is beneficial to eat this too, especially when the food has been organically grown.

We all have an instinct for this kind of choice, which may be developed to a greater or lesser extent. You may often find yourself intuitively attracted to food of a particular colour. For instance, when we need vitality we are naturally attracted to yellow and orange foods. When we need cleansing and detoxification we are attracted to green, which we are also drawn to when we lack minerals in our diet. When our brain lacks nutrition we tend to choose more dark or richly coloured foods. Red, orange and yellow foods on the whole have a more alkaline effect; blue, indigo and violet foods tend to be more acidic, and green foods are more pH neutral.

Studying the subject and experimenting with your diet will help you to develop these healthful instincts further, and teach you how to listen to what they say to you. Further understanding of the effects of different coloured foods will be gained by familiarizing yourself with the qualities of the distinct coloured rays described above, and from sources of more specialized references listed in the Appendix.

RED ENERGY IN FOOD

When we need the energy of red, such as when we are run down or anaemic, we are often in need of foods rich in iron (iron oxide is red); these are also generally cleansing foods, and contain high levels of potassium, which give vitality and stimulate the root chakra. These include:

strawberries
red apples
plums
cherries (both so-called black and red)
watermelon
red peppers
beetroot and their tops
radishes
currants (both black and red)
red meat.

Other foods that are not red in colour but which contain this
energy are:

> spinach
> leeks
> cress
> watercress.

ORANGE ENERGY IN FOOD

Orange foods are rich in enzymes which aid digestion, and
provide us with vitamins which particularly strengthen our
energy and give us vitality. They often also boost the
immune system. The list includes most orange-skinned or
orange-fleshed vegetables and fruits, such as:

> oranges
> mandarins
> tangerines
> clementines
> kumquats
> apricots
> mango
> papaya
> peaches
> cantaloupe melons
> orange peppers
> pumpkin and squash
> carrots
> swedes
> egg yolks
> those wonderful immunity-enhancing bee products –
> honey, bee pollen, propolis and royal jelly.

Yellow-coloured foods are especially called for when we need to work on the functions of the solar plexus chakra, or detoxifying the liver and gall bladder – as we know, the colour yellow is closely associated with these organs, as seen in jaundice – or for detoxification in general. These foods are often mildly acidic in content, and are essential for maintaining a well-functioning digestive system. All yellow fruits and vegetables are excellent for this purpose, including, for instance:

   lemons
   grapefruit
   melon
   pineapple
   sweetcorn
   yellow sprouts
   butter
   egg yolks
   products of the evening primrose.

GREEN ENERGY IN FOOD

Foods that are green help strengthen the heart system and associated functions of the heart chakra. They are excellent for cleansing the blood and helping to drain the lymphatic system. All green plant food, except those that are over-acidic or over-alkaline, are helpful in this way. As green is the balancing element of the spectrum of colour energies that sustain us, it seems reasonable to ensure that green foods form the centre of our diet – whether we are vegetarian, vegan, carnivorous, omnivorous or just very fussy!

BLUE ENERGY IN FOOD

Foods from the remaining end of the colour spectrum tend to be less abundant and varied than the ones we have looked at so far, and so it is easy to overlook them. Nonetheless, they are still vital to our health and well-being. Blue foods are helpful for the cooling and calming functions that have been mentioned in association with the blue ray, above, and include:

> blueberries
> bilberries
> blackberries (which are often really a deep blue or violet)
> black grapes
> damsons and other wild plums such as sloes
> fish, veal and asparagus.

INDIGO ENERGY IN FOOD

Foods carrying indigo energy serve similar purposes to those that are blue, with an additional value for the nervous system, brain and other higher human faculties. Foods listed above for blue or below for violet can be used when any of the functions of the brow chakra require energizing.

VIOLET ENERGY IN FOOD

Violet is required by the pineal gland, crown chakra and all their associated functions, and for the nourishment of our spiritual aspect.

Blue to violet foods, too, are often rich in magnesium and other elements which are vital to mental and brain functions. Violet foods include:

> blackberries
> purple grapes
> purple broccoli

red cabbage
aubergines
beetroot.

– put another way, these are the foods which have almost
moved round to the red end of the spectrum again.

USING COLOURED LIQUIDS

This method of colour healing is probably one of the most
ancient we have; it is certainly known to have been used for an
extremely long time in India, and is still used in some of the
smaller Indian villages. It is very easy to use, and safe in that it
is a gentle method of absorbing a particular colour energy into
the system. With coloured liquids, there is no need to use the
balancing complementary colour.

The basic method is to introduce the effect of a colour into a
liquid, commonly either water or honey, using direct sunlight
which has passed through a colour filter of the required hue.
You can do this for yourself at home: simply work out from the
information above which colour you need, and then use
coloured gels accordingly. Place the liquid in a container with
the coloured filter over the top, and leave in the open or on a
windowsill to absorb sunlight, including some direct sunshine
if at all possible, as this potentizes the fluid. This process is
called solarization.

If you use water, choose pure water or spring water and
leave it for about an hour in strong sunlight (in summer), or
several hours (in winter). The water will keep fresh in a refrig-
erator for up to three days, and should be sipped throughout
the day. Water charged with the red/orange/yellow end of the
spectrum will not keep as well as that which is imbued with
blue or violet. Because of its active effect, the red/orange/yel-
low water should preferably be drunk in the morning and

avoided at night, or you may not be able to sleep. Likewise, the blue or violet product can be drunk in the evening or at night, and will indeed help with insomnia. Coloured glass bottles can be used as an alternative to coloured gels.

If you are using honey, it can be left for three days and nights, in which case it will also absorb the light of the moon as well. Honey will keep the colour properties much longer than water, and can be taken at the rate of one spoonful a day. It should be stored in a cool, dark place. Some authorities suggest that milk, sugar and other liquid or food substances can be colour solarized too.

CHAKRA DRINKS

These are drinks made from specific fruit and vegetable sources which will help to strengthen weakened or damaged chakras. The drinks listed here are based on apple juice, with a range of other appropriate active ingredients for you to choose from. These are especially beneficial during the winter months, when our systems rely on reserves of energy that have been absorbed during the warmer and more light-filled months of the year. A juicer is very helpful for making them at home.

Root Chakra Drink

To the base of apple juice add beets, strawberries, raspberries, lemon or orange. A vegetable drink can be made using beets and tomatoes, with celery or fennel added if desired.

Sacral Chakra Drink

Add carrots and oranges to the apple base. For a predominantly vegetable drink, add carrots and celery to the apple juice base.

Solar Plexus Chakra Drink

Grapefruit, lemon and pineapple in addition to apple – excellent for cleansing, and very tasty. You can also add a banana to apple juice, with a squeeze of lemon.

Mix celery, fennel and apple for a high potassium drink. Or you can mix fennel with lemon and apple.

Heart Chakra/Throat Chakra Drink

Mix apple juice with lemon and blueberry. You can add banana or orange as well if you wish.

Brow Chakra/Crown Chakra Drink

This drink will serve for both these chakras. Combine apple with bilberries, blackberries or purple grapes. These dark fruits are all excellent sources of magnesium. To make it richer you can also add yoghurt and honey.

Rainbow Chakra Drink

This will stimulate all of the chakras and help to promote maximum vitality and well-being. It is made by combining fruits from each colour. You could mix apple with orange, pineapple, fennel, white or red grapes and blueberries or blackberries. For a vegetable version, try tomato with carrot, lemon, fennel, celery and basil. This one is also rich in a wide variety of vitamins and minerals.

COLOUR IN CLOTHING

Although this is, strictly speaking, beyond the scope of a book on colour healing, you can apply the same principles of the use of colours in choosing colours to wear to being further health and benefits. For instance, you could choose colours to wear to benefit certain chakras or corresponding zones in the body, or to help remedy certain ailments (*see pages 57–63*). Or you might wish to choose to wear clothing that enhances certain emotional or psychological states (*see pages 21–24*).

COLOUR IN YOUR ENVIRONMENT

Likewise, some of the principles in this book can be used to choose beneficial colours to surround yourself with, such as in the decor of your home or workplace, whether for physical health or psychological health benefit. The sections to refer to are as mentioned above for clothing.

INNER METHODS OF COLOUR HEALING

Now let's look at some methods of applying the same principles in a less physical but none the less equally powerful way. These are ways of internalizing colour and the healing energy that is available to us from it. These methods may be new to you, but if you practise them regularly you will find that they are actually very simple and straightforward, and can easily become second nature to you. Regular use of these techniques will produce the most profound benefits – improvements in your health and well-being, your knowledge of yourself and your ability to fulfil your greatest potential in life.

VISUALIZATION

Consciously using and training the mind to 'see' inwardly or to visualize in a particular way is an increasingly popular way to bring about personal transformation, and is used by people in an progressively wide range of situations. This method, a kind of meditation really, has been used in spiritual contexts for thousands of years, for instance by Buddhist monks and other sages and mystics, and is now thought highly of by top-flight athletes and sportspeople and high-flying business executives. Called 'creative visualization' it is also a very widely practised method in the world of alternative health and mind-body-spirit pursuits. The basis of the technique is that whatever is created and held in the thoughts, whether consciously or unconsciously, whether with effort or by default, has much more of a tendency to become real to us in an outward way – in the state of our health, in the state of our emotions, in how we behave, and thus even in what kind of experiences we attract in life. Colour visualization is one possible way into this whole powerful field of possibilities. At its basis, then, it is about creating our lives the way we would like them to be. Even conventional medicine and conventional science are realizing how powerful the mind and the imagination can be, and what a major part they play in how we are – that we create our reality all the time with our thoughts, attitudes and ideas. When we are able to do this consciously, we naturally become more empowered and in control of our destiny.

Learning to visualize colours and see them with the inner eye, then, gives us access to another powerful tool for this process of creation. Doing it successfully often brings to the surface any resistance we may have about whether our lives can really change for the better, or whether indeed we are really worthy or deserving of having things the way we would really like them to be (whether this means enjoying vibrant good health or having happy, fulfilled and successful lives). If these kinds of inhibitions might affect you at first, continuing the practice with effort and dedication can bring the additional benefit of eroding these underlying, sometimes unconsciously held negative beliefs. This is in itself a profound process that will in turn bring all kinds of other benefits.

Practising inner colour visualization can help us to develop the ability to know how our different inner energies are, and

help us to understand any inner blockages of these energies and how to remove them, by either visualization itself or by other methods or colour healing. Colour visualization helps us to develop our overall intuitive sense for how we are and what we need at any moment. Following the guidelines below, based on the chakra system already described above, you can activate your creative mind and learn how to focus awareness within yourself. Many of us are not used to doing this – we may even have been taught since childhood that to look within in this way is weak, overly indulgent or self-centred. Our modern Western culture is very outwardly directed, very performance motivated, and far too quick to discard something that requires time and patience to develop. With this method, if you practise, you will develop the ability to look within with patience, learning to be gentle, non-judgemental and trusting of yourself and your healing processes. And the more you can develop these inner abilities, the less you will need to be dependent on purely external techniques of adjusting and balancing your energy fields.

The method we will use is based around the colours associated with the chakras, connecting them to the particular aspects of health, organ systems, emotional qualities, spiritual states and so on associated with each particular chakra. When you have got used to these associations and to seeing these colours inwardly, you will soon be able consciously to stabilize, energize or rebalance any of the chakras by the inner use of colour. In the course of this practice you may find, for instance, that there is one colour that you have particular difficulty in visualizing, let's say yellow. You may well be able to relate this difficulty to the emotional issues associated with yellow – perhaps to do with your sense of confidence, self-worth or personal power. You can then do something about this. (*See pages 22, 54 and 58.*)

Do persevere with these visualization exercises, even if you find them difficult at first; working with them regularly will help to bring all the chakras into a state of balance with one another, and you will eventually begin to notice an increased sense of well-being. And of course you can do them anywhere – while you are new to it, it may be best to do them somewhere peaceful and private, but once you are familiar with them you can even do a bit of colour work while sitting on the bus, or in the queue at the post office! In this way you will find you can use it any time you are feeling tired, low or out of sorts. Or if you are experiencing pain in a particular part of your body, you can visualize the colour for that zone and let the vibration and frequency of that colour give you the healing energy you need, even if it is only a temporary relief until you can see a health practitioner or take another form of direct action yourself.

If you have difficulty seeing the colours with your inner eye, you can use a visual aid at first. Pieces of coloured paper or cloth will do fine – focus on one colour at a time, perhaps the one that you have most blockage with visualizing, and look at it from time to time during your visualization. You can also look at this colour at other times during the day. As you look, have the sense of slowly absorbing that colour into your consciousness. Eventually it will become 'anchored' into your mind, so that you can call it up at will and see it quite vividly in your mind's eye.

COLOURS AND ZONES OF THE BODY

During the course of your practice with colour visualization you can refer to the guide to the chakras (*see page 51–56*). What follows is a short summary of the colours as they relate to the zones of the body, and some additional examples of specific applications of specific colours in visualization.

As you visualize any colour you can also focus your attention on the corresponding part of the body, to increase the benefits of this form of meditation.

Red	used in connection with the root chakra, energizing the very lowest portion of the abdomen and also the hips, legs and feet
Orange	the colour of the sacral chakra, feeding energy into the abdomen and lower back
Yellow	resides in the area of the solar plexus chakra, which is below the sternum and over the stomach
Green	relates to the heart chakra, and the chest area; pink is also associated with this zone
Blue and turquoise	the throat chakra
Indigo	the brow chakra
Violet	the crown (top of the head) chakra.

Specific applications

- A bad back could be helped by visualizing the colour of the corresponding chakra zone of the spine (green for the upper back, yellow for the mid-back, orange for the lower back), but it is also a good idea to visualize a rainbow of colours pulsing up and down your spine. This can help open the flow of energy and break up blocks of tension that congest the natural flow all along the entire spine. Do this while lying flat on your back on a firm surface, with your knees drawn up and a book under your head to straighten the spine.

- Sore legs will respond well to visualizations using red and green.

- For alleviating a headache, imagine blue, violet or green in your head, and orange or red in your lower back. This can be helpful because headaches are often due to excessive energy held in the head, and this will help to restore the vertical balance of energization.

- Liver problems, often related to unresolved emotional problems such as anger, rage or hatred, can be helped by using violet, green or gold.

- Gold is also useful, along with green and pink, for people with heart problems, and for those who get weak or vulnerable easily or are susceptible to suffering from other people's problems.

- Gold and silver can both be used to protect any physically weak or vulnerable area.

- Menstrual cramps, which correspond to congestion in the root chakra zone, can be helped by alternating visualizations of red with those of green.

Colour visualization is not a cure-all for severe physical conditions, but it can relieve pain and discomfort, stimulate healing energies where needed and enable you to do something substantial for yourself, as an adjunct to health treatment from a qualified practitioner.

MEDITATING WITH COLOUR

Colour meditation is a wonderful way to put colour healing into practice at a very profound level.

When we look within with this method we are slowly beginning the process of detaching ourselves from the purely material

world around us and our personality or how we appear to others in the world, connecting instead to that part of ourselves which is permanent, indeed eternal. This is what is traditionally known in spiritual matters as the greater Self, or the I AM – the aspect that transcends gender, age, nationality, profession, wealth or any outward action. This Self is reflected well by the essence of colours. By developing your meditation skills you bring your more worldly personality, with its daily identification with temporal problems, into contact with the larger, all-knowing part of your soul. The benefits are greater tranquility, more peace of mind, more positive and joyful attitudes, and increased detachment from the effects of physical or emotional pain.

Meditation is a method of going within yourself which calms the mind and restores vital, subtle energies to the system. Colour meditation in particular helps you to deal with the particular emotional qualities and life experiences that are associated with each colour, and with the corresponding chakra. These emotional qualities can be either positive or negative. The colour red, for example, is associated on the one hand with patience, stability and security, and on the other with violence, destruction and lust. All these feelings, in fact, have an order and purpose in our lives, even though some of them can have a dysfunctional effect when taken to extremes or when not dealt with properly. Using colour meditation can help you to come to terms with and heal the dysfunctional effect of these more negative qualities, and strengthen the role of the positive ones.

So to continue with our example, if you have an imbalance in the root chakra, the one associated with the colour red, you may experience an unsettled quality in the feelings associated with it, or you may even sense a problem in the root chakra as you become more sensitive and attuned. This imbalance may be disruptive and chaotic in its effect, undermining many aspects of your life. You can strengthen the balance of the root chakra by meditating on the colour red and its positive emotional qualities. Some schools of colour meditation also provide a particular geometrical shape to visualize (for more on this, see the Appendix). Rebalancing the root chakra in this way will help you to build a much stronger foundation for your affairs, as this chakra has particular resonance for this aspect of our total makeup.

THE COMPLEMENTARY COLOURS

Another way to use colour meditation is to employ the effects of complementary colours (*see page 15*). So if the root chakra is adversely affected and its energies damaged by the sort of dysfunctional emotional effects mentioned, it will also be helpful to work with green, the complementary of red. This will help bring in the qualities of love, friendship and peace, for instance.

In this kind of way colour meditation can help us access the very colours we need, providing a natural and organic form of healing for all the levels of damage in our lives, enabling the whole energy field to become balanced, clear and powerful, and restoring vitality and peace in our lives.

MEDITATIONS ON THE SEVEN CHAKRA COLOURS

The form of meditation presented here has been developed to help you focus your awareness inwardly in the context of the vibrational dimension of colour. You can proceed with it at your own pace; some will move quickly to a more or less instantaneous possibility of rebalancing, while others will move more slowly and at a more profound level to open the doors to connection with the I AM within.

To prepare for this practice choose a place where you will be able to concentrate for some time, undisturbed by the telephone or other interruptions. Sit in a comfortable position which you will be able to maintain during the meditation, with your back

straight. Alternatively you can lie down, but not if it will cause
you to fall asleep; you need to maintain a degree of alertness.
Have your eyes partly closed, looking down towards the tip of
your nose. If you wish you can play some peaceful music, or you
may prefer simply to enjoy the silence. As with colour visualization, you may wish to use visual aids to recall colours at first.

Take several slow, deep breaths, and release any tension that
you can feel in your body. Inwardly scan round your body for
any tense spots, paying particular attention to the joints – the
areas around the hips, knees, neck, elbows and wrists. Also
consciously let go of any tension in the major muscles of your
legs, buttocks, arms, shoulders and back by breathing deeply
into your chest and inwardly instructing the muscles to let go.
You may want to try tensing up each set of muscles briefly,
before letting go. This feeling of relaxation and openness greatly enhances the healing and benefits of the meditation.

Red: the Root Chakra

Focus your awareness on the base of your spine. Visualize the
colour red filling this area, encompassing the breadth of your
hips. Imagine the intensity of red radiating down your legs,
through your knees, calves, ankles and feet. Then sense it
spreading down through your toes and into the soles of your
feet, and connecting from there down into the earth. Now focus
on the following emotional qualities:

- *Patience:* the emotional attunement we can have to the
  rhythms and pulses of time as we experience them in the
  physical world

- *Structure:* this symbolizes the structure of your life
  and the boundaries that give your life meaning and
  purpose

- *Stability:* this permits you to manifest your higher reality here on the earth plane

- *Security:* the quality of safeness you need in order to let your life unfold and evolve as it should

- *Manifestation:* the ability to make your dreams come true

- *Order:* the harmony you need in order for your life to work

To seal the chakra symbolically with light, visualize a cross of light within a circle of light. You can do this at the end of each chakra meditation, or to wrap up a series of meditations on various colours.

Orange: the Sacral Chakra

Bring your awareness up from the root chakra to the sacral chakra, located about 2 inches (5 cm) below your navel and about 2 inches (5 cm) into your abdomen. Visualize the colour orange radiating around this area, around the pelvic bone and into the organs of this zone – the reproductive organs, kidneys and intestines. Visualize the colour nourishing the soft part of your belly, easing any tension that you might be holding here, which can limit your experience of sensuality and pleasure. Also visualize it radiating backwards, into your lower back and sacrum; this area symbolizes your ability to move forward and into the flow of life. Allow the vibrant sense of this colour to intensify, and focus on the following emotional qualities:

- *Pleasure:* your ability to sense joy and feel at ease within your physical body

- *Sexuality:* focus intense energy into your genitals and other erogenous areas of the body; this lets you embrace and celebrate your sexuality, and gives you freedom to express this part of yourself

- *Well-being:* the attainment of an optimal sense of feeling good about yourself and enjoying life. This is located in the sacrum area of the lower back; dysfunction in this emotional area accounts for a great deal of lower back pain

- *Abundance:* this is your connection with the flow of goodness, available to you when you open yourself to life, perhaps taking the form of prosperity or of health, friends or love; abundance means having a full life

Yellow: Solar Plexus Chakra
Bring your awareness to this chakra, located over the stomach and just under the breastbone or sternum. Visualize yellow filling this upper abdominal area, as bright as the sun at midday. Explore its emotional qualities:

- *Self-worth:* this represents the core of how deeply you value yourself: it is the quintessential determinant of how loving you are to yourself

- *Self-confidence:* the quality which comes when you know how good you truly are: it reflects your trust and love for yourself

- *Empowerment:* this means projecting your worth onto the world; you know who you are and what you can do to effect change and maintain yourself in the world in the way that you feel good

PRINCIPLES OF COLOUR HEALING

PRINCIPLES OF COLOUR HEALING

- *Choice:* the ability to choose freely what is for your highest good and greatest joy

Green: the Heart Chakra

Bring your awareness up to the central area of the upper chest, and back towards the middle shoulder blades. Visualize green light radiating through this area, and also out into your arms and hands. It represents the pure light of love, which connects you with all life. Focus on these qualities in turn:

- *Love:* the centre of your emotional life, just as the heart is the centre of your physical body; life is learning the significance of love

- *Brotherhood:* this comes from the centre of your soul, and is that part of you which is connected to all people

- *Friendship:* this is when we share our hopes, dreams or even fears with others; we become deeply united in a bond of friendship with those whom we open ourselves to

- *Peace:* the quality of radiant harmony which comes when we learn to accept life and open our hearts to it

Blue/Turquoise: the Throat Chakra

Bring your awareness to the centre of the throat, and visualize turquoise filling the area between your jawbone and the base of your neck, also encompassing your mouth, teeth and tongue, and the spinal column in your neck. Intensify your sense of this colour and let it radiate deep into your throat, easing any tension in the base of your skull or in your neck or jaw. This chakra is blocked in many people, who fail to express their feelings

PRINCIPLES OF COLOUR HEALING

appropriately or else express deeply suppressed emotion in a sudden, uncontrolled outpouring. Here are some of the related emotional issues:

- *Will-power:* this allows you to harness your energy for living and working; it helps you to control your energies and permits you to use them in ways that can bring you happiness and pleasure

- *Creativity:* creative expression comes from combining the emotions of the heart and the thoughts of the mind; life is creative by its very nature; owning your creative energy brings consciousness of your unlimited potential to create your life the way you want it to be

- *Communication:* expressing your thoughts and feelings; essential for your physical, emotional and spiritual survival

- *Listening to the truth:* this is your ability to listen to, and recognize, the truth of your inner needs, personal desires and inner thoughts; being receptive to your inner truths puts you in touch with the greater truths of life

Indigo: the Brow Chakra

Bring your awareness up to the point just between your eyebrows, and visualize an intense indigo light radiating outwards from this point; the intensity of light from this centre fills your eyes, ears, sinus cavities, mouth and brain. Then open yourself to the emotional and energetic qualities of this chakra:

- *Wisdom:* the quality that comes when you have distilled the essence of your life experiences and refined your perceptions about yourself

- *Discernment:* this is your ability to know what is for your greatest joy and highest good

- *Imagination:* the quality you need for seeing the best things in life for yourself

- *Intuition:* your inner knowing which gives you information and signals about people, places and things; using it can enrich your life and help you to find the inner guidance you need for your journey through life

Violet: the Crown Chakra

Now bring your awareness up to the very top of your skull, and visualize a beautiful violet light shining from this centre. Feel this colour covering your whole body, like a long cloak which gives you protection, healing and tranquility whenever you need it. Then open yourself to the gently and innately spiritual qualities of the crown chakra:

- *Serenity:* this is an aspect of your higher Self which is always available whenever you surrender to the present moment, and which fully accepts you just as you are

- *Bliss:* the rejoicing which comes when you accept your higher Self and are deeply connected to that part of yourself

- *Beauty:* this comes with acceptance of what is; it is only through acceptance that you can see the beauty in all things and all people

Practising these meditations, if done regularly, will strengthen and fortify your own energy, make you more aware of

88   yourself, and enable you to distinguish yourself and your
own energy patterns from those of other people. You can
meditate upon one chakra in particular or all of them in turn.
As you practise you will find the process becomes easier,
more natural, almost effortless. You can also combine colour
meditation with other forms of meditation that you already
use or are interested in.

APPENDIX: RESOURCES AND USEFUL ADDRESSES

BOOKS

Mary Anderson, *Colour Therapy* (Thorsons, 1990)

R. M. Evans, *Introduction to Colour* (Wiley)

Theo Gimbel, *Form, Sound, Colour and Healing* (C. W. Daniel, 1987)

—, *Healing through Colour* (C. W. Daniel, 1988)

—, *Colour Consciousness* (Hygeia, 1991)

—, *The Colour Therapy Workbook* (Element, 1993)

—, *The Colour Healing Book* (Gaia, 1994)

J. W. von Goethe, *Theory of Colour* (1810)

D. B. Judd and G. Wysxecki, *Colour in Business, Science and Industry* (Wiley)

Marie Louise Lacey, *Know Yourself through Colour* (Thorsons, 1989)

C. W. Leadbetter, *Man Visible and Invisible*

Jacob Lieberman, *Light: Medicine of the Future* (1991)

G. Oeri, *Man and His Images* (Studio Vista)

Rita Robinson, *Colour Your World* (Newcastle Press, California)

H. & D. Sun, *Colour Your Life* (Piatkus)

Ambika Wauters can be contacted at:
15 Whaley Lance
Whaley Bridge SK12 7AE
Tel: 01663 735 288

Gerry Thompson can be contacted at:
42 Stanford Road
Brighton BN1 5DJ
Tel: 01273 206 000

Theo Gimbel can be contacted at:
Hygeia Studios
Brook House
Avening
Tetbury GL8 8NS
Tel: 01453 832150

INDEX

infra-red light 7, 44
Infra-red Thermography 37–8
inhibitions, overcoming 58
initiative, taking 57
inner methods, of colour healing 74–88
innocent, protection of 55
insomnia 42, 61
instinct 15–16, 47
intellect 50
intestines 58
intuition 56, 87
    and aura recognition 51
    and choice of colours 47
    development, through colour visual
        ization 76
Inuits 41
iron 67
itches 61

jet lag 25, 42
joints, stiff 36

kidney infections/disorders 58, 62
Kilner, Dr W.J. 38
Kilner screen 38
Kirlian photography 38–9, 49–50, 49
Kirlian, Simyon 39
knowledge 56
Krakow (scientist) 25

Lacey, Marie Louise 34
lamps:
    with colour filters 31
    healing 64
language, colour expressions 16
learning disabilities 42
Leavy, Dr 40
legs 78
lethargy 57
libido, low 57
light:
    absorption and reflection 13–14
    colour as medium for perception and
awareness of 9–12
    patterns of 56
    physical response to 17, 19, 25, 30
        see also Seasonal Affective Disorder
light blue 21–2

light-based technology xii, 44–5
light-based therapy 35–42
light-metering functions 56
lights, coloured, healing with 64–5
limbic brain 17
lines:
    blue or black, and depression 50
    brown, and miserliness 50
liquids, coloured 71–3
liver:
    detoxification 69
    problems 5, 58–9, 79
love 50, 55, 85
low blood pressure 57
low vitality 10, 57
lung problems 58, 61
Luscher Colour Test 21
Luscher, Prof Max 21, 43
lymphatic draining 59, 69

McDonald, Dr Sharon 36
magenta:
    in colour analysis 14
        maximum exposure time 65
        therapeutic effects 63
magnesium 70
magnetic colours 14–15
marketing 19–20
Massai 2
matching, of energies, through choices 11
Matraya School of Healing 34
meditation 74, 79–88
medium, for perception and awareness of
    light 9–12
melatonin 19, 40, 41
memory, cellular 31
menstrual cramps 58, 61, 79
mental health 20, 43–4, 62–3
migraine 10, 37
milk, colour solarization 72
mind:
    broadening 58
    subconscious 34
    unconscious 31
misers 50
moods 11, 19, 56
moon goddess 2
music therapy, for back problems 31

PRINCIPLES OF COLOUR HEALING